Comparative Performance Measurement

Elaine Morley
Scott P. Bryant
Harry P. Hatry

Comparative Performance
Measurement

THE URBAN INSTITUTE PRESS
Washington, D.C.

THE URBAN INSTITUTE PRESS
2100 M Street, N.W.
Washington, D.C. 20037

Library of Congress Cataloging in Publication Data

Morley, Elaine.
  Comparative Performance Measurement / Elaine Morley, Scott P. Bryant,
and Harry P. Hatry.
        p. cm.
Includes bibliographical references and index.
  ISBN 0-87766-700-4 (paper, alk. paper)
  1. Organizational effectiveness—Evaluation. 2. Performance
standards. I. Bryant, Scott P. II. Hatry, Harry P. III. Title.
  HD 58.9 .M67 2001
  658.4'013—dc21
                      00-012505

Printed in the United States of America

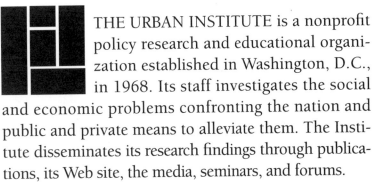 THE URBAN INSTITUTE is a nonprofit policy research and educational organization established in Washington, D.C., in 1968. Its staff investigates the social and economic problems confronting the nation and public and private means to alleviate them. The Institute disseminates its research findings through publications, its Web site, the media, seminars, and forums.

Through work that ranges from broad conceptual studies to administrative and technical assistance, Institute researchers contribute to the stock of knowledge available to guide decisionmaking in the public interest.

Conclusions or opinions expressed in Institute publications are those of the authors and do not necessarily reflect the views of officers or trustees of the Institute, advisory groups, or any organizations that provide financial support to the Institute.

Contents

Exhibits

Preface

This book is primarily intended for practitioners—public managers and employees at all levels of government—looking for ways to improve the services provided by their organization or agency. Managers and employees of nonprofit, service-providing organizations, which often function in ways similar to government agencies, are also part of this audience.

This book also should be useful to members of advocacy and community groups and those looking for better ways to understand or communicate the issues their organization is focused on and determine the effectiveness of efforts to address those issues.

The information presented here also should be of interest to elected officials, who have ultimate responsibility for services provided in their jurisdictions, and citizens, who are the owners, funders, and often customers or recipients of public and nonprofit sector services. Elected officials and citizens who are looking for better ways of understanding what agencies are accomplishing and more effective means of accountability should find this report useful.

We thank the Alfred P. Sloan Foundation, particularly Ted Greenwood, for supporting the comparative performance measurement effort undertaken by the Urban Institute that provided the basis for this work. We also acknowledge the work of the International City/County Management Association's (ICMA) Comparative Performance Measurement Consortium. The work of the Consortium jurisdictions and ICMA Consortium personnel contributed significantly to the development of the ideas expressed in this report. The ICMA team included Michael Lombardo, Barbara Moore, Evelina Moulder, and Louise Snyder. Gerald E. Newfarmer and Amy Cohen Paul of Management Partners, Inc. were part of that team. Additional Urban Institute team members were Daryl Herrschaft, Mary Kopczynski, and Shelli Rossman. We acknowledge the efforts of the jurisdictions participating in the Consortium and jurisdictions participating in other comparative performance measurement efforts, whose experiences have been tapped for many of the examples and suggestions included in this work.

We thank reviewers of various drafts of this work for their helpful suggestions, including Jay Fountain of the Governmental Accounting Standards Board; Michael A. Pagano, professor and director of graduate studies, Miami University; John Shirey, city manager, Cincinnati, Ohio; and an anonymous manuscript reviewer. We also thank our Urban Institute colleague, E. Blaine Liner, for his advice, support, and review of an early draft. Although we appreciate the contributions of those noted above, the authors acknowledge their responsibility for any errors herein.

Elaine Morley
Scott P. Bryant
Harry P. Hatry

Chapter 1

By its focus on results or outcomes, CPM can help communicate to the public an agency's accomplishments and performance in comparison with similar agencies.

What Is CPM, and Why Is It Important?

An explosion of effort in performance measurement by all levels of government in the United States, and internationally, has occurred in recent years. In addition to the public sector's increased interest, the private nonprofit sector has also demonstrated growing interest in performance measurement. As agency staff collect data (and, frequently, report it on the Internet), they—and citizens they serve—have begun asking how their agency is doing as compared with other similar agencies. This has led to what will become a major aspect of the information about agency performance—how agencies "stack up" against other similar agencies.

Comparative performance measurement (CPM) can be used to improve the management and operations of a particular agency or function, to improve policy and resource allocation decisions, and to communicate to the public what is being accomplished and what community needs should be addressed. In particular, CPM involves

- measuring the performance of an agency, jurisdiction, or area of concern,
- obtaining performance information from similar agencies or jurisdictions,
- comparing the performance of the agencies, operations, or jurisdictions,
- identifying differences in performance and the reasons for these differences,
- learning from these differences how performance can be improved, and
- applying what is learned.

As a rule, CPM should follow internal performance measurement and comparison of performance among different geographic or functional divisions of the agency.

This is largely because a clear understanding of performance within an agency is prerequisite to comparing its performance with other agencies. The remainder of this chapter discusses why CPM is important, describing how it builds on other public management initiatives and identifying potential pitfalls.

How Can CPM Be Used?

Public sector agencies face several inherent challenges as they seek to improve outcomes and provide more effective and efficient services. First among these barriers is the lack of any real competitive pressure. Second, it is often difficult to measure and communicate what is being accomplished by public sector agencies and to create a sense of public accountability. Third, the public sector has limited substantive research available as to what works in achieving meaningful results. The role CPM can play in addressing these is discussed in the following sections.

CPM as a Motivator for Improved Performance

One of the most substantial barriers to effective management and service delivery in the public sector is the lack of competition. In the private sector (and many other endeavors of life, such as athletics, the arts, and even academic achievement), competition drives innovation and product or service improvement. Private companies compete both in terms of quality and price. Consumers determine which products provide the best value—the best quality at the best price. Those products determined by consumers to be the best value achieve comparative advantage and succeed, while products of poor value quickly fade away.

It is difficult to motivate real improvement in public sector services without these competitive or market forces. Public sector agencies are typically free from the pressures of achieving and maintaining comparative advantage. Increasingly, however, some public agencies face the possibility that substantial portions of their work will be contracted out, or privatized. CPM sends the same kind of signals the marketplace provides for private sector goods and services. By comparing the performance of similar agencies, CPM creates similar competitive pressures.

CPM can also serve to motivate improved individual performance. Public sector employees, like most people, can be motivated by competition. However, it is often difficult to communicate to employees their agency's purpose, accomplishments, and performance. CPM can help demonstrate how well employees are performing compared with others. In particular, an agency's performance compared with others can serve as a basis for recognizing the employees of that agency. It can also spark the competitive spirit of agency employees as they strive to outperform other agencies. The performance levels of other better-performing agencies can be used to establish targets for improvement. CPM can also be effective in identifying issues or barriers to improved performance, in identifying ideas and solutions to those issues or barriers, and in communicating to employees that service is an important element of what an agency does.

CPM as an Accountability Tool

Another substantial barrier to effective public sector management and service delivery is the difficulty in clearly measuring and communicating what is being accomplished, and how well. This task is important in creating accountability to elected officials and the taxpayers who support government services, as well as to the customers who are direct recipients of those services.

Public sector accountability is at best indirect. Consumers can indicate their degree of satisfaction or dissatisfaction with public sector services through voting or choosing whether or not to live or operate their businesses in a certain city, county, or state. However, these decisions are infrequent, difficult to tie directly to individual agency performance, and may often send mixed messages about conflicting consumer objectives.

The advent of performance measurement, especially when outcome information is reported regularly in an understandable way, has been a major step forward in demonstrating accountability for results. CPM can build on performance measurement and add another dimension to accountability—comparisons among similar agencies.

By its focus on results or outcomes, CPM can help communicate to the public an agency's accomplishments and performance in comparison with similar agencies. Furthermore, through development of common customer survey questions and instruments, CPM can be used to compare the satisfaction level of citizens or customers with the services provided by different agencies.

CPM as a Tool for Determining Best Practices

Much less recognized is the fact that CPM is a powerful tool for assessing what does and does not work. Industries that have achieved remarkable improvement have done so by identifying and implementing "best" practices. The medical field, as an example, has focused on comparing the performance of different approaches and treatments, and applying what is learned to improve service quality. The automotive industry has emphasized comparing the safety performance of various vehicles and safety devices (using both test and actual experience data). The resulting information has then been used to identify best practices and substantially improve the quality of today's cars.

Government and nonprofit agencies can follow this model. CPM can provide the base of information for analysis, determining what factors lead to better performance. While substantial differences usually exist among agencies delivering similar services, typically there are more similarities than differences. For example, local police departments throughout the United States operate in basically the same way. Each deploys field officers to patrol and respond to citizen calls and detectives to investigate crimes. While these police agencies may operate in different environments (such as different demographic settings), considerable similarity exists as to their missions, organizational structures, and activities. By using CPM to identify the most successful agencies, the best or most effective practices can be identified and shared.

What Does CPM Add to Public Management Improvement Efforts?

CPM builds on other public management improvement efforts, including performance measurement, privatization, managed competition, and Total Quality Management (TQM). Each of these is discussed in the following sections.

Performance Measurement

Performance measurement, although in use for several decades, has only recently become a common tool by which the public sector can better understand and communicate what it is accomplishing. Historically, the public sector has focused on inputs and activities, paying less attention to the outcomes or results achieved by those inputs, activities, programs, and strategies. Today, the focus is shifting much more to what is actually being accomplished.

As public sector organizations and agencies implement performance measurement, they compare their current and past performances. Some are also setting targets against which future performance will be compared. These comparisons demonstrate real progress in public sector management. However, such comparisons provide little information on achievable results or new approaches to or methods of improving performance.

By comparing its performance with others, an agency can determine how much improvement can be made and gain new ideas. CPM provides this outside comparison. For example, an agency may be celebrating a reduction in the amount of time required to process client applications—from an average of 10 days to 8 days. This may be an achievement well worth celebrating, but until the organization compares its new performance level with similar agencies, it has only a partial picture of what can be accomplished. Similar agencies may be processing client applications in just 2 days. However, comparisons of such indicators should be made with caution, since the quality as well as the speed of service may differ.

Privatization and Managed Competition

Privatization of public sector services attempts to subject public sector services to the pressures of private competition and take advantage of the benefits that such competition brings—improved quality and efficiency. However, many of the services provided by the public sector are unique, and it is often difficult to adapt them to a competitive marketplace.

Privatizing such services may mean the provider is a private sector company, but may not create competitive pressures and the associated benefits. Additionally, services delivered by the private sector, many of which are provided for the "public good," can potentially be compromised or lost. Fortunately, CPM has the potential to provide the motivational benefits of privatization. Comparing performance among similar agencies creates competitive pressure for increased quality and efficiency.

Managed competition has been an effective way of bringing private sector competitive pressure to bear on those public sector services that are the same as or similar to services provided in the private sector. In its most common form, managed competition pits a public sector organization and its employees against private sector contract providers. For example, a public sector organization and private contractors may each bid on collecting trash from a certain area of a city, providing janitorial and building maintenance services for a public building, or providing landscaping maintenance for a public park. The work will be well defined in a set of bid specifications and awarded to the lowest bidder, whether public or private sector.

While managed competition offers substantial benefits, its application is very limited. Many of the services provided by the public sector are unique to the public sector. Managed competition can be applied only to those services the private sector currently provides or can be enticed to deliver.

CPM does not have these limitations and can be applied to most public agencies and services. While CPM may not create the same competitive intensity, it has the potential to generate substantial competitive pressure. Additionally, where services *are* provided by a private contractor, CPM can be used to determine if the contractor is doing a good job.

Total Quality Management (TQM)

TQM focuses on determining the cause of poor product quality within an organization and working to substantially reduce or eliminate those causes. TQM relies heavily on a detailed understanding of the processes involved in providing a service or accomplishing a result. This effort uses such analytic tools as statistical process control, work flow analysis, cycle time reduction, system redesign, quality function deployment, and benchmarking.

CPM can be used to identify areas in need of improvement—where the tools of TQM can most effectively be applied.

What Are the Potential Limitations of CPM?

As is true of any tool, comparative performance measurement has its limitations. Perhaps the most significant of these is the fact that no two jurisdictions or organizations are completely comparable. Each has unique characteristics and situations that make it different from all others. As a result, it is impossible to find organizations that are exactly comparable. Therefore, effort should be put into identifying those that are "roughly" comparable—those that are most similar to each other. Unique features then become factors potentially explaining differences in performance, approach, or method.

Another key limitation is that CPM, like any tool, can be misused. In many cases, comparisons have been incomplete, used poor quality data, or were biased to support a particular point of view. To be useful, CPM must be conducted as thoroughly and carefully as possible. Valid comparisons, even if rough, require substantial effort and commitment.

A third limitation is that the process of determining performance indicators for comparison, identifying comparable agencies, collecting and checking performance information, and analyzing and reporting the comparative information requires a substantial amount of time, effort, and money. These costs should be well understood prior to undertaking a CPM effort.

Fourth, CPM data, like performance measurement data, do not in themselves explain why performance is different—why the results are high or low, good or bad—relative to other organizations. Before assumptions can be made about performance, the reasons for high and low performance levels must be examined. These reasons include:

- Factors not accounted for in the CPM effort that might have caused a high or low level of performance on an indicator. Examples are unusually good or bad weather, new state or federal requirements, major changes in resources, regional or demographic differences, and changes in clients being served.
- The data for a particular agency may not conform exactly to the data definition used by other agencies or the CPM data collection effort. Even with the most rigorous effort to collect consistent data, such variations will inevitably occur.

The final limitation is the concern that an agency will be identified and reported as performing less well than other similar agencies. This assessment could have a negative impact on the agency and could make the agency, or others, less willing to measure and report performance.

The Focus of This Book

This book focuses on public sector, interjurisdictional CPM efforts. It is primarily intended for practitioners—public managers and employees at all levels of government—looking for ways to improve the services provided by their organization or agency. Managers and employees of nonprofit, service-providing organizations, which often function in ways similar to government agencies, are considered part of this audience. Nonprofit service organizations, encouraged by such national associations as the United Way of America and by their funders, have begin using outcome measurement. National associations of nonprofits and their members are beginning to develop common data elements for

CPM purposes in order to encourage improvements and identify successful practices. This is likely to become an area of considerable growth for CPM.

Chapter 2 discusses the different types of and approaches to comparative performance measurement, with numerous examples. The remaining chapters explore establishing the scope of a CPM effort in terms of what to compare (chapter 3), preparing for data collection (chapter 4), collecting performance information and making it comparable (chapter 5), analyzing the results of the effort (chapter 6), reporting the results (chapter 7), and applying the information (chapter 8).

Chapter 2

CPM efforts range from those that are mandated or initiated by others to those that are self-initiated, cooperative efforts.

Types and Examples of CPM Efforts

CPM efforts are initiated for a number of reasons. Some are mandated by federal or state governments, with the lower levels of government required to track and report their performances. In other cases, governments themselves have initiated CPM efforts in order to improve the services they provide and results they achieve. However, CPM efforts are not only initiated by governments. Some journalists believe comparative information on the results of public sector efforts will be attractive to their readers. Advocacy groups, such as those focused on child welfare, the environment, or similar issues, use comparisons to focus the public's interest and efforts on the areas with the most severe problems.

While each CPM effort has its own unique characteristics, this book groups them into four categories:

- consumer-oriented comparisons
- advocacy group comparisons
- mandated reporting and comparisons
- self-initiated cooperative comparisons

The first three categories can be viewed as "external" CPM in that the agencies whose performance is measured are not involved in initiating the effort, and they may not play any active role in some of these efforts. In contrast, cooperative comparisons involve active agency participation. These categories, while not meant to be an exhaustive list, are discussed in the following sections. A final section identifies and discusses the characteristics of and differences among types of CPM efforts.

There are many CPM efforts under way (some long-standing, others relatively recent) that cannot be explored in detail here because of space limitations. Because of its focus on *inter*jurisdictional CPM efforts, this book does not address *intra*jurisdictional CPM efforts, such as the work of the Fund for the City of New York's Center on Municipal Government Performance, which develops comparative data for neighborhoods within that city (see Additional Readings). Nor does it include efforts to promote performance measurement that are not comparative in nature.

Consumer-Oriented Comparisons

Any of the current product shopping guides is essentially a compilation of performance indicators and a comparison of how each product performs on the indicators. A good example is any one of the new car shopping guides that have become so popular and are nearly essential for purchase decisions. Most of these do well in defining performance indicators that judge the new models and providing information on how each model performs. This information can be invaluable to consumers who want to compare specific features and determine the relative value of different models.

The federal government also is a source for comparative performance measurement of interest to consumers. For example, the U.S. Department of Transportation regularly reports on key air travel performance indicators for major domestic airlines and airports. Information is published monthly on such indicators as flight delays, mishandled baggage, overbooking, and consumer complaints (U.S. Department of Transportation 2000).

Consumer-focused comparative information also has a positive impact on the producers of consumer goods. Today's consumers are accustomed to comparing most of the products and services they use. This situation gives producers an incentive, or perhaps more accurately, creates the necessity for improved product quality and value. This leads to new management and operational processes, expanded creativity and innovation, and a fairly continuous effort to improve product quality.

It is not surprising, then, to find that book and magazine publishers are interested in providing information to citizens on overall community conditions, which are based in part on services commonly provided by the public and non-profit sectors. Some of these consumer-oriented comparisons focus on "quality of life," which is measured by a number of factors and is partly the result of public sector efforts. The *Places Rated Almanac* (IDG Books) and *Money* magazine's annual ranking of the "best places to live" provide such information. Each establishes a series of factors and indicators for comparison and ranks locations based on these factors and indicators. While these rankings do not directly compare the performance of agencies or jurisdictions, many of the indicators are affected by services provided by the public sector. However, such rankings cannot be viewed as direct indicators of the quality of service provided by a particular agency. Additionally, some publications report data for entire metropolitan areas, thus blending data related to agencies in multiple jurisdictions that compose that area.

Some consumer-oriented comparisons focus on specific services provided by the public sector. Education is one area that has received particular attention in recent years. Two commercially developed efforts focused on higher education include *U.S. News & World Report*'s comparison of colleges and universities and *Business Week*'s comparison of business schools. Similarly, many states have begun making available performance data for public school districts, and many school districts provide comparative data for individual schools. Such data tend to generate considerable media coverage and public interest. Because of this, comparative education data often prompt corrective action in poorly performing schools or school districts. A discussion of educational CPM is included here with consumer-oriented data because of high levels of public interest in this data. However, many efforts to collect and disseminate comparative data are focused as much or more on educational officials as on the general public.

Caution should be exercised when using comparative data compiled for commercial purposes. Comparisons generated primarily with public appeal in mind may not always be performed as rigorously as would be desired. Publishers do not always identify their sources of data, or even the years the data represent, and the data for a given report are not always drawn from the same time period. Popular publications may not always provide an adequate explanation of how different factors are weighted or combined to arrive at rankings.

The following sections provide examples of consumer-oriented CPM efforts focused on overall community ratings, education, and health care.

Places Rated Almanac

The *Places Rated Almanac* (Savageau and D'Agostino 1999) has been published regularly since 1981. It provides information about and rankings for many U.S. and Canadian metropolitan areas (354 were included in the 2000 edition) in nine quality-of-life categories, including health care, crime, housing, education, and the arts. For most of these categories, a number of indicators are compiled into an overall rating. For example, in health care, the number and quality of hospitals, the number of doctors, the availability of specialists, and the availability of emergency medical services are combined to arrive at a rating, which is then compared with ratings of other locations. Other categories use a single indicator. The crime category, for example, compares "crimes committed per 1,000 population" for each location. Each area's crime rate is then used to determine its rank.

The information in the *Almanac* is compiled from existing sources. For example, the crime information is collected from the Federal Bureau of Investigation's (FBI) annual report, *Crime in the United States*. Similarly, job and employment information is obtained from data provided by the Bureau of Labor Statistics. The value of the *Places Rated Almanac* is that all the information related to quality of life is put into one report and used to rate and rank different areas.

While the *Almanac* provides valuable basic information for consumers as they rate the quality of life in their areas or others, it has several key limitations. The first is its somewhat arbitrary assumption that each of the categories is of equal weight in determining the rankings. In reality, the value of each category will vary widely depending on the individual.

Another limitation of the *Almanac* is the way in which some of the factors are designed. For example, the crime rankings consider all reported crimes equally and rank each area based on reported crimes per 1,000 population. In reality, different crimes have different levels of severity and a greater or lesser impact on the quality of life in a given area. In the *Almanac*, an area that has a high murder rate but a low rate of property crimes may actually be rated better than another area that has a high rate of property crimes but a low rate of murders.

Similarly, recreation and arts rankings are based on the sheer number of recreational and artistic/cultural opportunities in an area, without any adjustment for the actual number of people or the quality of the opportunities. As a result, the larger metropolitan areas, such as Los Angeles and New York, always rank high in these areas. While these areas have substantial recreational and artistic resources, several million people use or compete for these resources. The *Almanac* does not make any adjustment for this. Furthermore, all the indicators used to rate health merely measure the availability of health services and resources, not the quality of care or the resulting health of the population (e.g., incidence of communicable diseases).

Money *Magazine's* "Best Places to Live"

Like the *Places Rated Almanac*, *Money* magazine annually ranks America's 300 largest metropolitan areas on a series of quality-of-life factors (*Money* 2000). These "best places to live" factors are grouped into nine categories:

- weather
- crime
- housing
- education
- cost of living
- health
- arts
- leisure
- transportation

Unlike the *Almanac*, *Money* magazine determines its criteria and their relative value or weight based on the results of a nationwide poll of its readers. In this poll, people are asked to rank 44 quality-of-life factors on a scale of importance ("ignore" to "very important"). The results are then used to weight the ratings and calculate an overall rank. The factors and rating procedures may vary somewhat from one year to the next.

The "best places to live" effort also produces several other rankings. Metropolitan areas are grouped by region, including the Midwest, the Northeast, the West, and the South. Additionally, within each region the areas are ranked with areas of similar size, using the categories of "large," "medium," and "small." This reduces the problem of comparing vastly different areas, such as Los Angeles, California, with Manchester, New Hampshire.

The information used in the *Money* rankings is from existing sources, including crime statistics from the FBI, water and air quality measures from the Environmental Protection Agency (EPA), and housing prices from the Association of Chamber of Commerce Researchers.

The *Places Rated Almanac* and *Money* magazine provide a starting point in comparative performance measurement, as well as motivation for some agencies to examine their priorities and operations and determine if better performance can be achieved.

U.S. News's *"America's Best Colleges"*

U.S. News ranks America's colleges because it believes a college education is one of the most important and costly investments students, families, and society will ever make (Lemann 1999). Therefore, students and their families should have as much information as possible about the comparative merits of colleges and universities. *U.S. News* groups U.S. universities and colleges into national and regional categories. Each is then ranked based on a weighted set of criteria, including:

- academic reputation—determined through a survey of officials at similar institutions
- student selectivity—based on a number of factors related to admissions
- faculty resources—based on quality and availability of faculty
- retention rate—based on the freshman retention and graduation rates
- financial resources—determined by the average educational expenditure per student
- alumni giving—based on the percentage of alumni donating to the university or college
- graduation rate performance—the difference between the actual graduation rate and the rate expected from entering test scores and educational expenditures

Each year, *U.S. News* sends an extensive questionnaire to each college. Returned surveys are checked and compared with data from other sources. Data collected through the survey are then checked or supplemented with information from the U.S. Department of Education, the Council for Aid to Education, the National Collegiate Athletic Association, the American Association of University Professors, Wintergreen/Orchard House, and previous *U.S. News* data.

The ranking provides detailed information on each university and college for each of the factors. Schools are ranked with similar institutions, such as national or regional universities, and national or regional liberal arts colleges. Regional schools are further grouped by location (north, south, midwest, and west). The top 25 percent of schools in each category are ranked numerically. The remaining schools are listed alphabetically within tiers. Second-tier schools are immediately below the top 25 percent, followed by the third and fourth tiers. *U.S. News* also ranks the top 50 national universities, public national universities, and national liberal arts colleges. Additionally, by accessing the *U.S. News* Web site (www.usnews.com), individuals are able to specify particular criteria and conduct a tailored search and ranking based on their individual criteria and weights.

Business Week's "Best B(usiness)-Schools"

Business Week takes a different approach to rating and ranking the quality of the top 25 U.S. business schools, basing both entirely on the point of view of the consumers, which it defines as the students and the companies that hire them (Reingold 1998). *Business Week* developed extensive surveys to get the perspectives of these two groups. These surveys are sent to graduating MBAs as well as to companies that actively recruit business graduates. Student surveys ask about teaching quality, program content, and career placement. Companies are asked to assess graduates' skills and rank the schools on the overall quality and success rate of graduates in their organizations.

The rankings are based entirely on the survey results. An overall ranking is presented, as well as rankings in both the corporate and graduate polls. Each school's ranking from the previous year is also presented. The rating report, published annually, provides additional information about the schools, including the annual tuition, percentage of applicants accepted, and the percentage of female, international, and minority students.

Education Performance Assessment

Numerous states have begun testing student achievement and are reporting the results to the public. The intent of publishing such information generally is to inform education administrators at the state and local level, and to create and support local effort and pressure to improve the quality of education. In some cases, such as the Maryland example that follows, states may use CPM information in their budgeting or other decisionmaking that affects schools.

Under the **Maryland School Performance Assessment Program (MSPAP)**, which has been in use for six years, students are tested for their ability to perform tasks and solve problems (Argetsinger 1999a, b). Six areas are tested, including reading, writing, language usage, math, science, and social studies. The state uses results to identify those schools that will receive cash bonuses and those schools that should be targeted for possible state takeover. Exhibit 2-1, published in the *Washington Post*, shows recent (1999) test result data compared with previous years' scores.

The Maryland effort, as shown in exhibit 2-1, provides some explanatory information to help readers understand the differences among school districts, including information on the percentage of students with limited English and the percentage who receive subsidized meals (an indicator of the extent of low-income families in a given school district). These factors could impact the ability of students in a particular school or county to perform well on the assessment.

Exhibit 2-2 shows the best-performing elementary and middle schools based on MSPAP results. This ranking was prepared by the *Washington Post* for its article on MSPAP results and illustrates the attention paid by the media to CPM efforts on topics with high consumer interest.

EXHIBIT 2-1

Example of Newspaper Reporting on Educational Test Results

MSPAP Results

The following shows the composite index† of third-, fifth- and eighth-grade students who met Maryland School Performance Assessment Program standards in reading, writing, language usage, math, science and social studies.

	Limited English* (percent)	Subsidized meals** (percent)	MSPAP Scores						1998 statewide rank	1999 statewide rank
			1994	1995	1996	1997	1998	1999		
Allegany County	0.1	47.1	28.8	37.2	40.2	41.8	47.6	48.1	14	12
Anne Arundel	0.4	16.4	41.5	44.5	47.3	47.1	48.4	46.6	11	14
Baltimore	1.4	27.2	39.6	44.5	44.7	47.7	49.8	49.0	8	11
Calvert	0.2	13.9	38.9	48.8	49.0	53.8	53.8	52.5	6	6
Caroline	1.0	43.3	29.5	34.7	38.7	40.9	44.3	42.4	17	18
Carroll	0.4	9.2	48.1	51.1	55.3	55.3	56.4	55.4	3	4
Cecil	0.4	22.9	38.7	42.5	41.5	47.2	48.4	49.7	11	10
Charles	0.4	22.2	33.0	34.5	38.5	38.2	41.9	43.6	19	17
Dorchester	0.6	45.1	25.1	34.1	39.1	40.5	41.2	37.2	20	21
Frederick	0.5	14.4	46.3	54.5	54.2	53.1	53.1	52.4	7	7
Garrett	0.0	44.4	41.5	46.3	45.4	47.4	43.8	45.4	18	16
Harford	0.6	16.8	42.2	50.9	52.2	53.6	58.3	56.3	2	3
Howard	2.2	10.3	51.3	56.0	56.9	57.9	60.1	59.3	1	2
Kent	0.5	37.4	45.9	39.6	50.7	52.3	54.7	60.0	5	1
Montgomery	5.8	22.5	47.6	50.7	50.8	53.0	55.2	54.9	4	5
Prince George's	3.8	39.2	24.2	29.9	29.6	29.2	32.1	31.1	23	23
Queen Anne's	0.4	18.0	40.4	40.7	44.9	45.1	49.3	49.7	9	9
St. Mary's	0.6	22.1	38.1	45.4	45.7	46.7	48.8	47.8	10	13
Somerset	1.0	55.4	22.4	24.8	29.8	31.4	33.7	31.2	22	22
Talbot	1.1	27.7	39.1	38.0	46.5	41.4	44.7	40.7	16	19
Washington	0.8	26.2	35.9	40.7	43.9	47.0	48.3	51.0	13	8
Wicomico	1.3	37.4	28.3	30.2	33.6	35.3	38.2	40.2	21	20
Worcester	0.7	34.2	30.6	35.3	35.8	39.7	46.0	45.6	15	15
Baltimore City	0.6	68.4	11.7	13.8	13.5	13.8	16.1	17.0	24	24
State	**2.0**	**30.5**	**35.3**	**39.6**	**40.7**	**41.8**	**44.1**	**43.8**	**n.a.**	**n.a.**

† Average percentage of students scoring satisfactory or better in all six areas tested.

* Percentage of students who have a primary or home language other than English and who have limited ability to understand, speak, read or write English.

** Percentage of students who are eligible to receive free or reduced-price meals, a general indicator of how many students come from poor households, based on income and family-size guidelines set by the U.S. Department of Agriculture.

SOURCE: Maryland Department of Education.

EXHIBIT 2-2

Example of a Newspaper Article Ranking Schools by Test Results

MSPAP Results

The following shows the top 10 ranked elementary and middle schools according to their scores on the Maryland School Performance Assessment Program standards.

County	School	1998 score	1999 score	1998 rank	1999 rank
Elementary schools					
Anne Arundel	Bodkin	57.5	82.5	204	1
Baltimore	Timonium	77.0	82.0	18	2
Montgomery	Potomac	79.8	81.8	10	3
Montgomery	Cold Spring	88.3	81.6	3	4
Montgomery	Somerset	89.5	80.7	1	5
Montgomery	Wayside	72.3	80.1	47	6
Kent	Rock Hall	88.4	79.7	2	7
Montgomery	Westbrook	79.3	79.5	13	8
Montgomery	Bells Mill	79.4	79.4	12	9
Montgomery	Garrett Park	76.7	78.5	21	10

County	School	1998 score	1999 score	1998 rank	1999 rank
Middle schools					
Montgomery	Herbert Hoover	70.9	75.4	5	1
Montgomery	Cabin John	76.8	74.7	1	2
Montgomery	Thomas W. Pyle	75.2	73.4	2	3
Howard	Burleigh Manor	71.9	73.3	3	4
Baltimore	Sudbrook Magnet	70.8	71.8	6	5
Baltimore	Dumbarton	64.3	70.8	25	6
Baltimore	Hereford	70.5	70.5	8	7
Baltimore	Ridgely	67.9	70.1	14	8
Baltimore	Cockeysville	69.5	69.7	9	9
Howard	Glenwood	58.7	69.7	36	10

NOTE: To allow comparisons of individual elementary schools to others throughout the state, The Washington Post ranked the schools based on their overall MSPAP performance. The rankings are based on 834 elementary schools and 238 middle schools in Maryland. The Maryland Department of Education does not rank schools according to their performance on MSPAP tests because the exams are just one measure of school quality, and schools' performance on them may not indicate significant differences in school quality.

Source: Argetsinger (1999b). © 2000 The Washington Post, reprinted with permission.

Maryland Higher Education Commission Accountability Reports

In addition to ratings of higher education by popular magazines, some state governments are also comparing the performance of public higher education institutions in their states. For example, public colleges and universities in Maryland have been required to submit annual "performance accountability reports" to the Maryland Higher Education Commission (MHEC) since 1988 (Maryland Higher Education Commission 1999). This system was modified in 1996 to require reporting on each campus's performance on key indicators. The indicators used are intended to reflect quality, effectiveness, accessibility, diversity, and the efficiency/allocation of resources. Indicators reported vary somewhat by type of college (community college, four-year comprehensive college, and four-year research institution). Each campus is required to develop benchmarks, or goals, to measure its performance on each indicator. Following are some examples of indicators in selected categories:

- Quality indicators—include indicators based on surveys of students and employers conducted by MHEC on such topics as graduates' satisfaction with job preparation, satisfaction with preparation for transfer to four-year institutions (where applicable), and employer ratings of preparation of graduates for employment.
- Effectiveness indicators—include second-year retention rates (the percentage of first-time, degree-seeking freshmen who reenrolled one year after matriculation), passing rates for each academic field at the institution for which licensing exams

are conducted (such as nursing), and graduation or transfer rates to public four-year colleges.

- Access indicators—include the percentage of college students in the county (or service area, if larger than the county) who are attending that college (for community colleges); for four-year colleges, this indicator is the percentage of students attending that college who are Maryland residents.
- Diversity indicators—include the percentage of students who are African American, the percentage of students who are minorities, and the graduation rate of African American students.

MHEC prepares an annual report that provides indicator data for each college in a separate section, which enables readers to compare different institutions even though comparative data are not provided in the same tables. In addition to the data, each section includes narrative describing the institution's mission, significant trends affecting it, and a narrative assessment of its progress in achieving its benchmarks. In some cases, MHEC identifies concerns regarding specific indicators, which are included in this section, along with the college's reply.

Third International Mathematics and Science Study (TIMSS)

Education is of sufficient interest and importance to warrant *international* CPM efforts, too. Conducted during the 1995 school year, TIMSS was the largest and most comprehensive comparative international study of education ever undertaken, focusing on mathematics and science achievement (Schmidt and McKnight 1998; Takahira et al. 1998). The International Association for the Evaluation of Educational Achievement (IEA), a Netherlands-based organization of ministries of education and research institutions from member countries, served as the international coordinating body. The U.S. Department of Education's National Center for Education Statistics and the National Science Foundation supported the United States' portion of this effort. Previous IEA studies focused on reading literacy (1992) and computers in education (1993).

The TIMSS effort was made up of three components, each focused on students at one of the three stages of schooling: midway through elementary school (3rd or 4th grades), midway through lower secondary school (7th or 8th grades), and at the end of upper secondary school (12th grade). Forty-one countries participated in the first component, 26 countries participated in the second, and 23 in the third component.

The comparisons for the third component focused on four broad areas of performance:

- Mathematics general knowledge—for all students in the final year of secondary education
- Science general knowledge—for all students in the final year of secondary education
- Advanced mathematics—for students in the final year of secondary education who had taken or were taking advanced courses in mathematics
- Physics—for students in the final year of secondary education who had taken or were taking physics

Both public and private school students participated in mathematics and science general knowledge assessments that contained multiple choice and free-response (open-ended) items. All tests were given in the primary language of instruction for each country. Additional information was collected, including student experiences in and out of school, school policies and practices, and an analysis of mathematics and science curriculum guides and textbooks.

The TIMSS effort differs from many other CPM efforts in that TIMSS data are being analyzed to determine the relationship between various educational factors and students' performance on the knowledge assessments.

Health Care CPM

Like education, comparative data for health care are also of considerable interest to consumers (Gormley 1998; Gormley and Weimer 1999). Due to the complexities associated with health care CPM and the evolving nature of this form of CPM, this topic is not addressed in detail here. However, some observations about health care CPM are provided below.

Comparative indicators for different kinds of health care providers, such as hospitals, HMOs, and nursing homes, have occasionally been developed by a variety of sources. These are sometimes referred to as "health care report cards." Consumer-oriented publications, such as *Consumer Reports* and *U.S. News & World Report*, have published such comparisons for the general public. One federal agency, the Health Care Financing Administration, had compiled annual hospital report cards but discontinued this practice in 1993, in part due to concern about the limitations of the data used. State agencies in a number of states (particularly those with large populations) compile and make available at least some comparative information about hospitals, such as overall death (mortality) rates and mortality rates following specific types of surgery. One complicating factor in reporting data related to patient outcomes, such as mortality data, is that such data must be adjusted to make it comparable across institutions. This "risk adjustment" reflects variations in the health status of patients served by particular hospitals or other facilities. Various mathematical models may be used to perform risk adjustments, and the models can incorporate a range of risk factors or characteristics.

Mandated reporting and comparison of performance information will likely become the norm in the health care industry. For example, the Joint Commission on Accreditation of Healthcare Organizations (JCAHO) has already begun requiring hospitals and other health care organizations to report performance data as part of the accreditation process. Using this performance information, the commission, insurance companies and other third-party payers, and patients will be able to rate health care facilities and make decisions based on these data.

Advocacy Group Comparisons

The second category of CPM efforts includes those conducted by advocacy groups. Such groups often use CPM to focus the attention of the public, or their own efforts, on the most severe social problems.

The Annie E. Casey Foundation's Kids Count Data Book

The Annie E. Casey Foundation, a private charitable organization dedicated to helping build better futures for disadvantaged children in the United States, annually publishes comparative performance information related to children (Annie E. Casey Foundation 1998). First published in 1985, the annual *Kids Count Data Book* reports and compares the performance of all 50 states on 10 indicators related to children's quality of life, including the following:

- infant mortality rate
- percentage of low-birth-weight babies
- teen birth rate
- juvenile violent crime arrest rate
- percentage of children in poverty

Information is displayed so as to make it easy to determine the actual performance of each state on each of the indicators. Readers can also see how each state's performance compares with the national average, if its performance has improved or worsened since 1985, and by what percentage. The *Data Book* also provides additional background information that may help explain the results or provide insight into the potential causes of improved or worsened performance, including the number of children by age group, the percentage without health insurance, and social, economic, and child care indicators.

This information is intended to increase public awareness of the status of children and to assess trends in their well-being. Trend information can help the public to understand improvement or deterioration in the quality of children's lives and to evaluate the effectiveness of efforts to improve their lives.

Governing *Magazine's "Grading the States:* A Management Report Card"

Although not an actual advocacy group, *Governing* magazine is very much an advocate for effective and efficient government (Barrett and Greene 1999). Because it compares or grades state governments, it falls into the category of advocacy group comparisons.

Funded by a grant from the Pew Charitable Trusts, *Governing* magazine and Syracuse University's Maxwell School of Citizenship and Public Affairs began their effort to grade the states in 1997. First, they divided public management into the following five categories and developed evaluation criteria for each:

- financial management
- capital management
- human resources
- managing for results
- information technology

With these categories and related evaluation criteria in mind, the team developed and distributed a survey to each of the states. The responses to the surveys, along with supplemental information, were reviewed in detail. Additional information was also obtained from over 1,000 interviews with individuals inside and outside of state government. The actual grades were developed based on a consensus among the academics and journalists involved in the project.

Obviously, there are inherent difficulties in ranking or grading individual states because there are substantial differences in the challenges each state faces as well as the services each provides. Even so, ranking or grading provides valuable information to the elected officials and employees of each state, as well as to each state's citizens.

The effort will be repeated in 2001, with a similar effort focused on local governments completed in 2002.

Mandated Reporting and Comparisons

Mandated performance reporting and comparison is an important form of CPM. The U.S. government, as well as many state governments, has mandated reporting of certain performance information—in some cases for decades. For example, the FBI's Uniform Crime Reporting System (UCR) mandates that all state and local police organizations report the number of crimes committed in their jurisdictions by category. This information is reported annually in *Crime in America*, which lists crime rates for each jurisdiction but does not rank or otherwise compare these rates.

Similarly, most state governments require local school districts to report performance information, including attendance, dropout, and graduation rates. More recently, some states have begun requiring student achievement testing followed by the reporting of those test results. As education has increasingly become a more important issue, school districts are being compared in terms of their performance in these areas (examples of educational comparisons were discussed earlier in this chapter).

Mandatory reporting of health care information by hospitals is evolving through the work of the Joint Commission on Accreditation of Healthcare Organizations, as noted previously.

In recent years, there has been movement toward reporting indicators associated with multiple services, rather than just the services associated with a particular agency or department. These efforts are similar to consumer-oriented publications' efforts to rate places to live, although they place greater emphasis on indicators closely associated with government services. The information in government-initiated efforts is intended not only for citizens, but also for public officials responsible for service provision or oversight. Some mandatory CPM efforts in the United States and the United Kingdom are described below.

United Kingdom Local Authority Performance Indicators

The Audit Commission of the United Kingdom (U.K.) requires that local councils (local governments) collect and report information on a series of performance indicators (United Kingdom 1999). These indicators were initially developed in 1992 as part of the U.K. Citizen Charter initiative. Under this initiative, each council was required to publish its performance on specific indicators in local newspapers.

Since FY 1993–94, the information on performance indicators for all councils has been compiled and reported to show how councils compare with each other. The purpose of this report is to help citizens know how well their council is "doing its job" and to answer the question: "Is the money you pay for council services being well spent?" Citizens are encouraged to "use these tables and charts to compare your council with nearby councils and to see how your council compares across England and Wales."

Auditors conducted a limited review of the methodology councils used to produce their performance indicator information. In some cases, the information was revised based on these reviews. In other cases, the auditors expressed doubts about some councils' arrangements to produce the information as defined. Where this was the case, the information reported was so noted.

Performance indicator information is presented with councils ranked highest to lowest. However, a high rank is not always better than a low one. Interpreting the rankings requires an understanding of what each indicator is measuring, so the report also provides commentary on each of the indicators. This commentary describes each indicator and provides possible explanations for differences in performance.

The U.K. performance indicator effort continues to evolve. Each year the Audit Commission solicits feedback and suggestions from local councils, police and fire services, government departments, and a wide range of consumer and professional organizations. Based on this feedback, the Commission revises the indicators, their definitions, and its overall approach as necessary.

Vermont's Community Profiles

The State of Vermont Agency of Human Services (AHS) has published CPM reports called "Community Profiles" annually since 1995 (Murphey 1998, 1999). These profiles provide comparative information on how each of 60 communities in Vermont is performing on a series of outcomes and related indicators. (For this effort, a community is defined as the area served by a school supervisory union.) This information provides users with some tools for understanding how their community performs relative to other communities and the state as a whole. Additionally, the community profile serves as a means to track changes in performance over time.

Prior to implementing community profiles, the Vermont Agency of Human Services and State Department of Education had recognized that their success in meeting the needs of those they serve was interdependent. They further recognized that many of the outcomes each sought to achieve were complementary. Based on this understanding, these agencies developed a common set of "outcomes" or "basic conditions of well-being for children, families, individuals, and communities." In 1998, the Vermont legislature mandated reporting on regional progress toward specific outcomes, defined as:

- pregnant women and newborns thrive
- children are ready for school

- children succeed in school
- youth choose healthy behaviors

A set of indicators is presented for each outcome. For example, the outcome "children succeed in school" is measured by such things as attendance rates, percentage of students meeting standards, average SAT scores, and high school dropout rates.

The Agency's planning division collects, analyzes, and presents information detailing each community's performance on these outcomes and indicators. Comparative information for each indicator is provided in both tables and graphs. Data are presented for the community, the county in which it is located, and the state; multiyear information is provided when available. Community profiles are available in print and on the agency's Web site.

Although the Vermont effort is driven by state government agencies, much of the effort has been carried out through regional partnerships of human service and education agencies. In turn, many of these partnerships have begun using the community profiles to coordinate and focus their efforts.

Georgia's Community Indicators

The State of Georgia (1999) recently initiated a database of community indicators somewhat similar to Vermont's effort. The database is organized to provide information on eight "key community conditions," which are:

- demographic
- economic
- fiscal
- educational
- health
- environmental
- social
- civic participation

Data for one or more indicators present a general sense of each community's performance in that condition. For example, indicators for health are the infant mortality rate (number of deaths occurring in infants under age 1 per 1,000 live births), children immunized by age 2 (percentage who have received the full schedule of age-appropriate immunizations against specified diseases), number of physicians per 10,000 population, and number of licensed nursing home beds per 100 persons age 65 and older.

The database is maintained by the Georgia Department of Community Affairs and is accessible on its Web site (www.dca.state.ga.us/commind/guide.asp). Users can view one or multiple community profiles. Data are available for cities, counties, and consolidated governments in Georgia as well as Georgia as a whole and the entire United States. Indicator data are primarily derived from existing sources, such as state agency or federal data (e.g., U.S. Census data). Therefore, data in the profiles do not always cover the same time period. The initial report included data for 1998; however, users eventually will be able to examine data for multiple years.

In the future, the report will include a section on indicators of "selected local government services." This section will provide in-depth information on specific services, information that will change on a rotating basis.

North Carolina's Division of Women's and Children's Health

North Carolina's Division of Women's and Children's Health (DWCH), part of the Department of Health and Human Services, collects data on various performance indicators from each county's health department (Goldstein 1998; Wolfe 1998). The indicators and the process were developed jointly by county representatives and state officials. The indicators provide performance information to the counties and health districts (which oversee groups of counties), and are included as part of the department's contribution to the state's program performance budgeting effort. In particular, indicators are collected for women's preventive health, maternal health, and child health and immunization programs. Examples of specific indicators for women's preventive health programs include the adolescent pregnancy rate, the percentage of repeat teen pregnancies, the percentage of women with short birth intervals, and the out-of-wedlock live birth rate.

Each county provides data to the DWCH, which then makes the necessary calculations to derive the indicators. The counties are divided into four comparison groups, with the 10 largest counties designated as the urban group. The remaining counties are placed according to their location within the state into one of three geographically defined groups—western, central, and eastern. DWCH reports the comparative data to the county health departments and the divisions to which they report, and each health department sees only the data for their own comparison group.

The report shows each county's value and rank on each indicator against other counties in its comparison group. Counties are ranked in two ways—the *value* of the indicator data for the most recent three-year period, and its *improvement* in each indicator. Data are calculated to show improvement (or decline) expressed as a percentage increase or decrease. In addition, DWCH calculates a cumulative ranking for each county. The report also includes comparison group and state averages for each indicator. (Recently, however, DWCH decided not to include the performance of other county offices in its report to a county, but instead provides the overall state average and the average for the county's own comparison group.) In addition to giving data back to the counties, Division personnel review each year's data with the local departments. Counties are then expected to use their data to set targets for their next contract with the state.

The indicator data help inform state decisionmaking. Regional consultants (state employees) are notified about poorly performing counties so they can arrange to consult with these counties to help them improve performance. DWCH also uses the data to identify these counties for possible increased state involvement in the development of their annual contracts with the state. The state may also impose financial penalties, or fund alternative agencies, but only if the counties fail to make a good faith effort to perform, as is stipulated in their contracts.

Self-Initiated Cooperative Comparisons

There are numerous examples of government efforts to compare performance in order to identify specific areas on which to focus attention and apply better or more effective practices. Following are several examples that have gained some prominence.

ICMA Local Government CPM Consortium

Under the auspices of and with the assistance of the International City/County Management Association (ICMA), a consortium of cities and urban counties with populations greater than 200,000 was formed in late 1994 for the purpose of comparing performance (Bjornlund 1999; Bjornlund and Okubo 1999; ICMA 1998, 1999a; Kopczynski and Lombardo 1999). This project was initiated primarily because many managers wanted to compare their agency's performance with other agencies. The participants hoped to develop valid and useful comparisons, which could be used to identify service elements that needed improvement and to share effective practices.

Initially, 44 cities and counties participated, each sending a representative to an initial meeting. The group decided at this meeting to focus on four key areas that were common to all the participants—police, fire/emergency, neighborhood, and support services. In order to develop performance indicators for comparison, four technical advisory committees were formed, one for each service. These committees included managers or key personnel responsible for these services in each of the participating cities or counties. The committees met numerous times to select and define the specific services within each area for which performance would be compared and developed indicators for these services. Detailed definitions were created to facilitate, to the extent possible, the collection of comparable performance information. These indicators and definitions were then compiled into data collection templates, which were sent to each of the participating cities and counties for data entry. The templates included three types of performance indicators:

- *Outcome indicators,* which represent some aspect of the quality or result of the service. Indicators are provided for two types of outcomes: intermediate outcomes, which should lead to the end desired but are not themselves a result (such as service response time), and end outcomes, which are the anticipated end results (such as reduced incidence of crime).
- *Efficiency indicators,* which report the ratio of the outcome or output produced by, or workload of, the service to the amount of input applied by the government to produce the outcome or output. For some services, efficiency indicators are calculated primarily in terms of staff resources associated with the outcome. Dollars expended are used, however, to calculate a small number of efficiency or unit cost indicators.
- *Input indicators,* which reflect the amount of resources (dollars expended or amount of employee time) used to produce an outcome. Although these data

are of interest for comparing activity across jurisdictions, they do not provide information on performance or what was accomplished with the resources.

Performance indicator information from each of the participating cities and counties was compiled and analyzed. Reports were then prepared presenting the comparative data for each jurisdiction's performance in each of the service areas. Some effort was put into identifying explanatory factors that contributed to differences in performance among jurisdictions and into identifying practices that contributed to more effective service delivery (these aspects of the effort are described in later chapters).

The consortium effort is ongoing, with data collected annually. The number of cities and counties participating has increased, and smaller jurisdictions have been included in the effort. The service areas addressed have also been expanded to include an additional area of interest—youth services—which includes such programs as child protection and welfare, health, substance abuse, and mental health, as well as prevention and intervention programs, probation/parole, recidivism, and other indicators of community response to the needs of children and youth.

North Carolina Institute of Governments (IOG) CPM Project

In 1995, several large cities and counties, the IOG, the North Carolina League of Municipalities, and the North Carolina Association of County Commissioners initiated the North Carolina CPM project (Coe 1999; Few and Vogt 1997; North Carolina Local Government Performance Measurement Project 1997). This group formed a steering committee and hired a project coordinator. The committee then selected which city and county services to include in the effort, using three criteria:

- importance of the service to the jurisdiction's mission
- number of citizens affected or clients served
- services that were candidates for contracting out or privatization

The services selected were:

- police services—including patrol, investigations, and emergency communications
- solid waste collection—including residential refuse collection, household recycling, and yard waste/leaf collection
- street maintenance—including street maintenance and repair

As a starting point, the steering committee decided to focus on the seven largest cities in the state. The project coordinator met with groups of representatives from each of the selected service areas in these cities. These groups then decided on the most appropriate performance indicators for each service area and developed definitions for the indicators.

Early in the project, the participants discovered the difficulty of comparing costs among the jurisdictions because of differences in budget and accounting systems. The IOG, therefore, developed a cost accounting model to facilitate the collection of comparable cost information. Using this model, costs were captured in four categories:

- direct personal services and operating expenses
- indirect/central costs
- equipment costs
- facilities costs

Each of these cost categories, and the types of expenditures that comprised them, were defined.

As data were collected, some reported figures were outside the reasonable range for those elements. To make the data usable, the project coordinator telephoned or visited the jurisdictions reporting questionable information to clarify or revise the data.

Jurisdictions reportedly have used information generated by this effort to make changes in workload levels, work rules, staffing levels, and service provision approaches. In one city, the comparative information was used to confirm a policy position that provides a higher level of service at a higher cost. Another jurisdiction discovered that it was spending more than the average on sanitation services, apparently due to its policy of allowing sanitation workers to leave work after "a fair day's work." This policy was subsequently modified, resulting in savings for that department.

State Revenue Departments' Performance Comparisons

In the early summer of 1996, several state revenue collection agencies began assessing the interest in and need for a comparative performance measurement effort related to tax collection (Weeks 1997a, b). They initiated an effort that would be coordinated by the Federation of Tax Administrators (FTA). According to an FTA presentation, the purposes of this effort were:

- to build a valuable FTA service for all 50 states—a management resource
- to create a foundation for sharing innovative practices and learning
- to set the stage for further questions

Much of the impetus for developing the comparative performance measurement effort was a general dissatisfaction with the types of comparisons that had been previously performed. These comparisons had focused mostly on such indicators as "enforced collections per collector" or "total collections per full-time employee (FTE)" and were of limited value because of substantial differences in how departments operated and collected information or defined the indicators. Additionally, a focus on delinquent accounts and enforcement activity often led to inappropriate and overzealous efforts by revenue agencies.

The effort began by defining the major "strategic" business processes common to most, if not all, revenue departments, including taxpayer registration, collections, return and payment processing, and dispute resolution. For each, the process was generally defined, performance indicators developed, and key terms defined. A test data collection then was conducted, focusing on two specific processes—refunds and deposits. Data were presented, showing the performance of each participating state without identifying the state. A major effort was made to identify process improvements from the data.

The effort is currently expanding, with numerous states expressing interest in joining the project. The following steps are planned for the comparative effort:

- Update and refine current measures for all 10 participating states—move in "bite-size" increments.
- Strengthen FTA commitment to build voluntary compliance in each state.
- Expand definitions of measurement types.
- Develop a performance measurement training and education focus.
- Implement continuous improvement ideas.

Long Beach Police Department Peer Comparison

In the fall of 1992, the Long Beach (California) Police Department initiated the development of a strategic plan (City of Long Beach 1994). The purpose of this effort was to identify the current issues and potential future challenges facing the department and to develop strategies for meeting these issues and challenges.

A business approach that included two major phases, issue identification and strategy development, was used to develop the strategic plan. During the issue identification phase, information was collected from numerous sources, including area citizens, department employees, the city council and the mayor, previous studies and reports, and through an overview of current operations. This information was used to identify the department's strengths, constraints or weaknesses, and future threats and opportunities.

During the strategy development phase, the department's vision for the future was refined. Strategic issues were identified, discussed, and prioritized based on their impact on that vision. Numerous alternative strategies for addressing each issue were developed. Those strategies most likely to contribute to the department's mission were selected, and an implementation timetable was developed.

It is important to note here that competitive analysis is a common element in *private* sector strategic planning. Such an analysis includes comparing an organization's operations with those of its competitors or peers. This comparison provides important insights into an organization's strengths and weaknesses, product differences, and the changes necessary for an organization to remain competitive in the future. Since the Long Beach Police Department's operations are similar to those of other police departments in the state, comparing these operations provided insights similar to a private sector competitive analysis.

The Long Beach Police Department's peer group was defined as the 10 largest municipal police departments in the state. The peer comparison, conducted during fiscal year 1991–92 (July 1, 1991 to June 30, 1992), included a survey distributed to each of the other departments. Because of the importance of obtaining accurate information, one of two deputy chiefs from Long Beach and a deputy city auditor conducted site visits at each department. Comparisons were made for the "customer base" (population and community characteristics) and such departmental factors as resources, expenditures, and patrol, investigative, and support services.

The information collected in the peer comparison was used to identify areas of strength and weakness. Additional information was obtained from those departments that performed better than Long Beach, and this information was developed into strategies that were incorporated into Long Beach's strategic plan.

Characteristics of CPM Efforts

Following are several key characteristics of and differences among CPM efforts that should be considered.

Degree of Agency Involvement

The role of the agencies being compared is a key factor in their acceptance of the CPM results and, potentially, in the quality of the information collected. In some cases, agencies are not at all involved in the comparison effort, such as those included in the *Places Rated Almanac* and *Money*'s "Best Places to Live." In these cases, agencies and jurisdictions in the locations compared are likely to accept the results based on how well they fared in the rankings.

In other CPM efforts, the agencies being compared participate to varying degrees. Agencies may participate by providing information or responding to a survey. For example, for *Governing*'s comparison of state governments, a survey was sent to and completed by the governor's office in 49 of the 50 states. Similarly, for the *U.S. News* ranking of colleges and universities, much of the information was collected directly from the institutions.

Some CPM efforts are undertaken with considerable participation from agencies in determining focus areas, developing and defining indicators, and reviewing comparison results, in addition to providing data. Examples of this approach include the ICMA CPM Consortium and the North Carolina IOG CPM Project.

Time Frame (Ongoing vs. One-Time)

Many CPM efforts are ongoing, collecting information and reporting on performance annually. These efforts help agencies develop and refine data elements and definitions, data collection instruments and procedures, analytic procedures, and reporting formats. Ongoing efforts also allow for comparisons over time in addition to comparisons among agencies. Such comparisons can help identify agencies that have made improvements in response to previous ratings. Examples include the ICMA Consortium, the North Carolina Institute of Government Project, the Annie E. Casey Foundation's *Kids Count Data Book*, and CPM efforts performed by magazines (*U.S. News*, *Money*, and *Business Week*).

Other CPM efforts are one-time or ad hoc efforts and provide information to support specific decisionmaking. One example is the Long Beach Police Department's peer comparison, which was conducted to support development of the department's strategic plan. While such efforts provide less opportunity for analysis over time, they can nonetheless be very valuable.

Source of Data Used for Comparisons

CPM efforts obtain performance information from three sources. The first is existing published information; comparisons such as the *Places Rated Almanac* and "Best Places to Live" rely entirely on such information. These sources are likely to provide the least current information, relying on data that often are several years old.

Surveys are another source of CPM information—often used as one of multiple sources of data. Examples include *Business Week's* ranking of business schools, which relies on surveys of business school graduates and companies employing them; and *Governing* magazine's "Management Report Card," which collected its initial information through surveys. One of the indicator categories in Maryland's Higher Education Commission reports is based on surveys of students and employers. The ICMA Consortium has developed common citizen or customer survey questions for jurisdictions to use in developing comparable customer satisfaction information.

Agency records are a third source of CPM information. This information must be collected directly from the agencies, therefore requiring some level of agency participation. Each of the cooperative CPM efforts discussed here—the ICMA Consortium, the IOG Project, the state departments of revenue comparisons, and the Long Beach Police Department peer comparison—rely heavily on agency record information.

Focus on Outcomes or Activities and Resources

CPM efforts differ as to the focus of their performance indicators. Some efforts focus primarily on outcomes or results. For example, the Annie E. Casey Foundation's *Kids Count Data Book* concentrates on specific outcomes related to children, including such indicators as child death rates, teen birth rates, and the percentage of children in poverty.

In contrast, other CPM efforts focus on the level of resources available or expended in a particular area or to provide a particular service. For example, the *Places Rated Almanac* lists such indicators as the number of hospitals or recreational facilities in each location. However, it does not provide information on the quality or impact of those services.

Method of Reporting

The way in which CPM information is reported also varies among different efforts. In many cases, emphasis is placed on the ranking of agencies compared, with one being rated as best and others following as next best and so on. An example is *Business Week*'s ranking of business schools. The top 25 schools are actually listed from 1st to 25th. However, most CPM reports do not specifically identify or rank participants as best or worst. Rather, the agencies and their performances are displayed, making such rankings fairly apparent.

Another way to present comparative information is by showing the data for each agency as compared with the median or mean of the comparison group. The *Kids Count Data Book* presents information in this way, with each state's information presented separately, along with comparisons with the 50-state average.

Still another difference in reporting is the extent to which information explaining differences in performance is presented. Most CPM efforts provide little or no such explanatory information. Some efforts, however, such as the *Kids Count Data Book*, provide background information giving insight into the causes of different performance. Typical examples of background information include the number of children by age group, the number without health insurance, and social and economic indicators related to children. The Maryland School Performance Assessment Program and the TIMMS effort also include information to help explain performance differences.

The ICMA Consortium reports have attempted to provide specific information on factors that may explain differences in performance. This information includes notes discussing explanatory factors with each indicator compared, as well as statistical analyses showing the relationship between performance indicators and potential explanatory factors. For example, one chart demonstrates that average police response time to top priority emergency calls tended to be quicker in jurisdictions that had more police per square mile. This effort has also attempted to provide information on practices or factors that lead to better performance among those jurisdictions that appear to be achieving better performance.

These examples of different types of and approaches to CPM efforts, as well as the key characteristics and differences among the various efforts, provide useful information on how to structure and implement an effective CPM effort. Chapter 3 discusses establishing the scope of the CPM effort.

Chapter 3

Determining the Scope of the CPM Effort

It is better to have a few meaningful indicators than multiple poor ones, and it is preferable to concentrate on outcome indicators rather than resorting to easy-to-develop workload or input indicators.

This chapter focuses on establishing the scope of the CPM effort. This process involves selecting

- services or topics to be included;
- participants (*jurisdictions* or *agencies*) to be compared; and
- performance *indicators* to be used in the effort.

These components are closely related and may be performed more or less simultaneously. The type of effort being launched—whether internally or externally initiated—determines who makes decisions about scope. (See chapter 2 for a discussion of types of CPM efforts.)

For self-generated (cooperative) CPM, the participants themselves define the scope. Decisions about scope are likely handled by representatives of the participating jurisdictions or entities. If this is the case, decisionmakers should obtain input about the indicators and comparison agencies from key stakeholders in their jurisdiction (e.g., elected officials, agency managers, and other staff). Such input improves the quality of the decisions reached. In addition, participation by stakeholders generally increases their commitment to and support of the effort. The end result is greater acceptance and use of the data generated by the CPM effort.

For CPM efforts mandated by a higher level of government (state or federal), officials of that level of government establish the scope. Again, it is highly desirable that the agencies whose data will be collected participate in the selection of services and indicators since they are likely to be major users of the comparison findings. As noted above, involvement in these decisions should increase "buy in" for the resulting product.

For other externally generated CPM efforts, the entity initiating the effort makes decisions about scope. Advocacy group CPM might involve representatives of the organization's constituents, perhaps as members of an advisory committee formed for this purpose. Advocacy groups might also seek input or feedback regarding scope from their constituents through surveys or through their newsletters or public forums. The scope of CPM efforts initiated by the media is likely determined by the reporting and editing staff of the organization initiating the effort. The topics discussed below are generally applicable to external CPM efforts.

Which Services Should Be Included?

There is no "right" number or type of services for a particular CPM effort. Different factors influence the selection of services in different types of CPM efforts.

- For CPM efforts involving active participation by agencies (cooperative CPM), selection of services will likely be made by agency representatives. They will likely select services provided by those agencies or choose a comprehensive set of services typically provided by the jurisdictions or agencies participating in the effort.
- For external CPM efforts using available data, such as those performed by advocacy groups, or consumer-oriented comparisons performed by magazines or newspapers, the organization leading the effort selects the services. Selection is usually based on the interests of the organization and its constituents.
- Unfavorable media coverage or a high volume of citizen or customer complaints about a particular service may be the impetus behind service selection for one-time or ad hoc CPM efforts. Generally, these are efforts where an agency or jurisdiction seeks comparative data for its own services—usually from similar agencies or jurisdictions. Alternatively, an official's interest in a specific service area may drive the selection in such cases.
- Services that are believed to be high priorities among customers are often selected for cooperative or external CPM efforts. CPM efforts initiated by advocacy groups or the media often focus on indicators perceived to be important to the public.

Which, and How Many, Comparison Agencies Should Be Included?

Two factors inevitably need to be considered by all types of CPM efforts:

- Are the participating jurisdictions or agencies similar enough to assure reasonable comparability?
- Will the effort to obtain and analyze the data be manageable within the resources available?

Each is discussed below.

Choosing Comparable Agencies

Major criteria for selection include:

- size of population served, such as jurisdictions with populations above or below specific levels (e.g., those with populations of 200,000 or above), or number of customers (e.g., service agencies with fewer than 100 customers);
- type of community served—urban, suburban, or rural;
- type of jurisdiction or agency—municipal, county, state, or nonprofit;
- regional location—within a state or within the country;
- size of the service-providing agency—measured by number of employees or budget size; and
- community demographics—e.g., households with similar income distributions, population densities, ethnic characteristics, etc.

While comparisons have tended to concentrate on population size in determining CPM coverage, this factor may not be as critical to comparability of services as is commonly thought. Our brief analysis of the 1996 data sample provided by the ICMA CPM Consortium indicated that population size within a broad range did not significantly explain 12 outcome indicators representing such agencies as libraries and police, refuse collection, and highway departments. (Regression analysis was used to assess the degree to which population size was related to the magnitude of the outcome indicator.)

Inevitably, no set of agencies will look the same on all criteria. As discussed in a later chapter, providing explanatory information as part of the CPM effort reduces the problem of differences among agencies. This process helps address comparability by providing information on factors that may explain some of the performance variations. Although comparability of the agencies included in the CPM effort is often very important, dissimilar agencies can learn much from each other. For this reason, CPM efforts that seek to identify "best practices" through their comparative data should avoid emphasizing strict comparability. Best practice insights can be gleaned from dissimilar as well as highly comparable organizations.

Selection of comparable agencies is not an issue for CPM efforts that are comprehensive in scope. In particular, mandatory CPM efforts might require the participation of all agencies of a particular type in the jurisdiction covered by the mandating agency. For example, a state-administered CPM might encompass all county health departments or school districts.

Exhibit 3-1 provides examples of the scope of agencies and services covered by two well-known cooperative CPM efforts.

An issue particular to many CPM efforts is that the group of agencies covered may not reflect the range of values typical for a specific service or indicator, adversely affecting the usefulness of the comparative data. For example, only high-performing agencies may choose to participate in a given cooperative effort and, therefore, their indicator data may show much better outcomes than would occur if a more comprehensive group of agencies participated. Low-ranking agencies in such a group might be perceived as poor performers, but in reality they might be average or high performing if compared with all such agencies. Conversely, in an

Examples of Agency and Service Selection for Voluntary CPM Efforts

Local Government Comparative Performance Measurement Consortium

Jurisdictions participating in this ICMA-coordinated effort initially limited participation to ICMA-member cities or counties with populations of 200,000 or more (the lower population boundary of the city managers' group that originated the effort). This cutoff was established to ensure that service provision conditions and practices would be reasonably comparable across jurisdictions. The size limit was subsequently lowered to cities and counties with populations of 100,000 or more.

To keep the project manageable, the Consortium has limited its scope to the four major service areas considered to be important to both citizens and managers. These include police, fire, neighborhood, and support services. Neighborhood services include road maintenance, streetlighting, code enforcement, housing opportunities, and libraries. Support services include purchasing, fleet management, information technology, human resources management, and facilities management. Participating jurisdictions are not *required* to provide data in all service areas although it is encouraged, and most have been doing so. Inclusion of a fifth service area—youth services—is planned,

and indicators for that are currently being identified.

North Carolina Local Government Performance Measurement Project

This project was initiated by members of the North Carolina Local Government Budget Association and is coordinated by the Institute of Government at the University of North Carolina at Chapel Hill. The first phase of the project involved comparative data collection from seven large cities (with populations greater than 60,000). The second phase added seven large counties, and the third phase added 14 medium-sized and small cities and counties.

Steering committees for each phase of the project determined the scope of services to be included in the effort. Services selected had to impact a large number of citizens and be important to the jurisdiction's mission. In some cases, the possibility of contracting out or privatizing a service was a factor in service selection. The first phase included three services—police, solid waste collection, and street maintenance. Services added in the second phase were those primarily provided by counties—child protective and emergency medical services, jails, and inspection functions (such as building and environmental inspections).

Sources: Kopczynski and Lombardo (1999) and Coe (1999).

effort primarily including poorly performing agencies, a low-performing agency might be considered a good performer. This issue does not generally affect CPM efforts that are comprehensive in scope, such as mandatory state efforts that include all school districts or all hospitals, or national efforts that include data for all states.

Fitting the CPM Effort within Available Resources

Some cooperative CPM efforts establish fees for participation, addressing the need for resources as well as limiting the number of participants. CPM efforts can also adopt a phased approach to membership, keeping the scope of the effort consistent with resources available. This approach also enables the effort to gain experience with a relatively small number of agencies and work out the "bugs" (such as unclear definitions or instructions, programming errors, etc.) before expanding the number of agencies covered—which may be accomplished by changing the participation criteria. The ICMA and North Carolina efforts (see exhibit 3-1) used a phased approach, and in both cases, the number of services included in the effort also increased over time.

Which Outcomes and Outcome Indicators Should Be Included?

An initial decision involves the *types* of performance indicators to be included in the effort. Exhibit 3-2 provides definitions of types of indicators commonly used in performance measurement.[1]

EXHIBIT 3-2

Performance Measurement Definitions

- **Performance Indicator**: A specific numerical measurement for each aspect of performance (i.e., output or outcome) that is under consideration.
- **Input**: Resources (i.e., expenditures or employee time) used in producing an output or outcome.
- **Output**: Completed activity. Outputs refer to the amount of work completed by the organization (e.g., number of miles of road repaired or number of calls answered).
- **Outcome**: An event, occurrence, or condition outside the activity or program itself and of direct importance to clients and the public. The outcome indicator is a measure of the amount and/or frequency of such occurrences. Service quality, such as the timeliness with which the service was provided, is often an important aspect of outcome measurement.
  - **Intermediate Outcome**: An outcome that is expected to lead to a desired end, but is not an "end" in itself. Examples include service response time, which is of concern to a citizen requesting service but does not tell anything directly about the "success" of the service, or changes in client behavior expected to lead to an improvement in the client's condition (e.g., better health).
  - **End Outcome**: The end result that is anticipated or desired (e.g., clean streets or a reduced incidence of crimes or fires).
- **Efficiency or Unit-Cost Ratio**: The relationship between the amount of input (usually dollars or employee-years) and the amount of output, or outcome, for a program. An efficiency ratio can be expressed as either the amount of input divided by the amount of output/outcome or the amount of output/outcome divided by the amount of input. *Caution:* If the indicator uses outputs and not outcomes, an agency with a low unit-cost ratio can achieve that result at the expense of the quality (i.e., outcome) of the service.

Source: Adapted from ICMA (1999a).

Outcomes reflect the consequences of an agency's efforts. They provide information on events, occurrences, conditions, or changes in attitudes or behavior that show progress toward achieving the agency's mission and objectives. Information on outcomes is usually of greatest importance to customers and citizens.

CPM efforts should carefully distinguish between outputs and outcomes, but also separate intermediate and end outcomes.

- *Intermediate outcomes* have the advantage of occurring in the relatively near term, earlier than end outcomes. They also are more influenced by agency efforts. These outcomes are expected to lead to desired ends, although they are not "end" or "final" outcomes themselves.
- *End outcomes* are the desired results of the agency's efforts (or of particular programs in the agency). Some end outcomes occur relatively soon; others may occur years after the agency's services are delivered. The long-term nature of some end outcomes is one of the reasons for including intermediate outcomes among the performance indicators (Hatry and Kopczynski 1997).

Many organizations and their upper-level managers also are very interested in comparing their *efficiency* or *unit-cost ratios* (also described in exhibit 3-2) with those of similar agencies.

Once the types of performance indicators for a CPM effort are selected, specific outcome and efficiency indicators associated with various services need to be identified. Some of the same factors that influence selection of services are likely to influence selection of indicators, namely:

- For cooperative CPM efforts, representatives of the participating agencies generally will be involved in selecting indicators.
- Indicators of service outcomes that are believed to have high priority among customers may be selected for cooperative or external CPM efforts.

The choice of CPM indicators is usually driven by the known availability of data on the service and the likelihood that different agencies have reasonably comparable data. In some cooperative efforts, agencies might opt to include some new indicators for which many agencies have not previously tracked data. One example of such a decision is drawn from the ICMA Consortium's Fire Services working group:

- Not all of the jurisdictions in the Fire Services working group routinely compiled data on the spread of fires (for example, from the room of origin to other parts of the same building or to other buildings). However, members felt that such "flamespread" data were an important measure of fire department effectiveness in fighting fires and agreed to include several such indicators among their fire suppression indicators, with the expectation that more jurisdictions would begin to collect such data. These indicators were expressed as the percentage of structural fire incidents (for various types of structures, such as residential multifamily, commercial, and industrial structures) where flamespread was confined to the room of origin.

A key example of including new indicators in CPM efforts is the use of surveys to obtain data about customer satisfaction with various aspects of a service or customer use of particular services (see chapter 5). Since the use of customer surveys is not common to all agencies, inclusion of such indicators invariably requires new data collection for at least some CPM agencies.

Converting Outcomes into Indicators

Outcomes need to be converted into outcome indicators to make CPM data collection possible. Outcomes are often expressed in general terms, similar to mission statements or goals, such as "reduce teen pregnancy" or "increase public safety." Outcome *indicators* need to be expressed as a numerical value—such as a number or percentage (a proportion or rate)—that indicates progress toward achieving an outcome. For example, "the number of births per 10,000 teenage females" indicates progress toward the outcome "reduce teen pregnancy." Expressing indicators numerically enables collection of comparable data across agencies.

For CPM purposes, indicators often must be "normalized" to account for size differences among jurisdictions or number of customers served (this is discussed in greater detail in chapter 5). For example, crime rates are often reported as crimes per 1,000 population—which adjusts crime data to account for variation in population size.

Most agencies or organizations provide more than one service or program. Thus, multiple indicators are needed to fully capture the outcomes of key functions. Each indicator should measure an important aspect of agency outcomes. In addition, some indicators can also reflect characteristics of the quality with which services are delivered. This includes characteristics that are important to customers, such as the timeliness and accuracy of the assistance provided, condition of facilities, courtesy with which the service is delivered, and overall customer satisfaction.

Several considerations come into play when selecting outcome indicators. Exhibit 3-3 provides criteria for selecting indicators.

Determining the Number of Indicators

There is no "right" number of indicators for a CPM effort. The number will vary with the number of functions or services covered by the effort. A large number of key indicators (e.g., 10 to 15) may be identified for some outcomes, while others may have only a few. Participants in cooperative CPMs may wish to select what the group perceives as a manageable number of indicators, adding more indicators in future years. For external efforts, the number will likely depend on the indicators for which data are available and the criteria listed in exhibit 3-3. External efforts may also use a phased approach, adding more indicators as they gain experience.

CPM efforts should strive to be as comprehensive as possible in selecting indicators that represent major aspects of a given service, within limitations of available

Some Criteria for Selecting Outcome Indicators

- The *importance* of what it measures.
- The extent to which it might be *duplicated by, or overlap with, other indicators.*
- The *understandability* of the indicator.
- The extent to which agencies have *influence/control* over the values of the outcome. But do not overuse this criterion. Often an agency will have less influence over the most important outcomes, especially end outcomes. As long as the agency is expected ultimately to have some tangible, measurable effect on the outcome, the outcome indicator should be a candidate for inclusion—whether the effects are indirect or direct.
- The likelihood that agencies to be compared will have the needed data and will make it *available in a timely way.*
- The *feasibility and cost* of collecting the indicator. However, note that sometimes more costly indicators are the most important—and should be retained.

Source: Adapted from Hatry and Kopczynski (1997).

data and resources. Failure to include key indicators can affect the usefulness—and use—of CPM data. For example, an agency may have below-average performance in some indicators and perform above average in others. If only the former are included in the CPM, the agency will unfairly be perceived as a poor performer (or vice versa if only the latter indicators are included). Additionally, since agencies tend to focus their efforts on improving services that are measured and reported, aspects of service that are not included as indicators in the CPM effort may be neglected. Therefore, performance in those areas may actually deteriorate (Gormley and Weimer 1999, 9–10).

Exhibits 3-4 and 3-5 include examples of indicators used by the ICMA CPM Consortium and the North Carolina Local Government Performance Measurement Project, respectively. These two CPM efforts primarily focused on basic local government functions, such as police, fire, neighborhood, and support services, rather than social services (although the ICMA Consortium is in the process of adopting indicators for youth services).

Exhibit 3-6 provides examples of some of the indicators used in Vermont's Community Profiles CPM effort, led by the state's Agency of Human Services. These reflect outcomes associated with a variety of social service agencies and schools. *Outcomes* for this effort are expressed as conditions of well-being for children, families, and communities, such as "children live in stable, supported families." Several *indicators* reflect progress toward achieving each outcome.

Data for the Vermont effort are reported for 60 geographic regions in the state. These regions are served by a school supervisory union (similar to a school district) and typically include several towns. Data for the CPM effort are derived from school and town-level agency records. Data also are aggregated to the county level and reported by counties as well as by the 60 regions (Murphey 1999).

EXHIBIT 3-4

Illustrative Outcome Indicators Used by the ICMA Consortium

Police Services
- Number of Part 1 crimes per 1,000 population (deterrence/patrol)
- Average response time to top priority calls from dispatch to arrival (deterrence/patrol)
- Percentage of violent crime arrests that are juveniles (criminal investigations)
- Number of Part 1 crimes cleared per sworn full-time equivalent (FTE) staff member (criminal investigations)
- Number of Part 1 crimes cleared per $10,000 expenditure on sworn staff (criminal investigations)
- Number of traffic fatalities per 1,000 population (traffic)
- Number of DUI arrests per 1,000 population (traffic)

Fire Services
- Residential and multifamily dwelling structure fire incidents per 1,000 multifamily structures (community risk reduction)
- Rescues performed per 100,00 population (community risk reduction)
- Average time from dispatch to arrival for fire suppression calls (fire suppression)
- Percentage of commercial fire incidents where flamespread was confined to the room of origin (fire suppression)
- Number of firefighter injuries per 1,000 sworn FTEs (fire suppression)
- Average time from arrival on scene to delivery of patient at medical facility for calls requiring an advanced life support response (emergency medical services)

Neighborhood Services
- Percentage of lane miles assessed as being in satisfactory condition (road maintenance)
- Operating and maintenance expenditures per paved lane mile assessed as being in satisfactory condition (road maintenance)
- Number of complaints received about residential solid waste collection services per 1,000 individual residential accounts (refuse services)
- Number of streetlighting defects per 1,000 streetlights (streetlighting)
- Total operating and maintenance expenditures per streetlight maintained (streetlighting)
- Average number of days to replace a defective streetlight (streetlighting)
- Average number of working days from case initiation to initiation of administrative/judicial action for code violations resolved during the reporting period (code enforcement)
- Total number of new low- to moderate-income housing units completed with public financial assistance during most recent program year (housing opportunities)
- Number of low- to moderate-income households that received public financial assistance and purchased homes during the reporting period per 1,000 persons below the federal poverty level (housing opportunities)
- Annual circulation per capita (libraries)
- Attendance at library programs per 1,000 population (libraries)

continued

- Average library cost per item circulated (libraries)
- Annual circulation per total FTE (libraries)

Support Services

- Percentage of purchasing volume (in dollars) awarded to minority/women-owned businesses (purchasing)
- Number of new transactions by central purchasing office per central purchasing FTE (purchasing)
- Percentage of light fleet available for use by operating personnel (fleet management)
- Average fleet maintenance expenditures per mile: all vehicles (fleet management)
- Percentage of help desk calls resolved at time of call (information technology)
- Employee turnover rate per 100 full-time employees (human resources management)
- Number of employee grievances and appeals per 100 full-time employees (human resources management)
- Response time to emergency repairs (facilities management)
- Average expenditure per square foot for custodial services (facilities management)

Source: ICMA (1998).

Breakouts of Performance Indicators by Key Demographic Groups

This is an underused set of comparisons. Providing breakouts of performance indicators by key demographic groups (such as age, race/ethnicity, and income groups, and gender) increases the usefulness of performance comparisons. Such breakouts can help agencies identify which other agencies are serving specific customer groups particularly well. Breakouts also are likely to yield fairer comparisons, since the aggregate data comparisons may include jurisdictions with different proportions of each customer group. (An alternative approach to using such breakouts is to use the proportion of customers in harder-to-help group(s) as explanatory factors. The latter are discussed in chapters 4 and 6.)

For some services, other breakouts are also useful. For example, reporting comparative crime data by major "classes" or categories of crime (such as violent and property crime and misdemeanors) is quite informative. Similarly, fire rates can be compared separately for residential, commercial, and nonstructural fires. Both of these indicator breakouts are used by the ICMA Consortium effort (see exhibit 3-4).

A cautionary note: Avoid selecting too many breakout categories. While it is easy for those involved in developing indicators to identify several breakout categories for each indicator, this can be burdensome for the agencies that have to provide the data. Try to restrict breakouts to the two or three that are most important for each indicator. Exercising restraint in this area is particularly helpful in the early years of a CPM. Additional breakouts can always be added in later years, after participating agencies have become more familiar with the overall data collection procedures.

EXHIBIT 3-5

Illustrative Outcome Indicators Used by the North Carolina Local Government Performance Measurement Project

Police Services

- Number of UCR (*Uniform Crime Report*) total Part 1 crimes per 1,000 population (patrol)
- Average response time to high priority calls (patrol)
- Sustained complaints about patrol officers per 10,000 population (patrol)
- Cost per dispatched call (patrol)
- Dispatched calls per patrol officer (patrol)
- Percentage of Part 1 crimes cleared of those reported (investigations)
- Investigative cost per Part 1 crime reported to the department (investigations)
- Investigative cost per Part 1 crime reported to the department per Part 1 crime cleared by the department (investigations)

Emergency Communications

- Calls answered per telecommunicator
- Emergency 911 calls answered per 1,000 population
- Average cost per call answered
- Average number of seconds from initial ring to answer
- For calls dispatched, average number of seconds from receipt of call to dispatch

Residential Refuse Collection

- Tons per 1,000 population
- Cost per ton collected
- Tons collected per FTE (full-time equivalent employee)
- Complaints per 1,000 collection points
- Valid complaints per 1,000 collection points
- Percentage of eligible collection points participating in household waste recycling program
- Cost per collection point

Street Pavement Maintenance

- Number of centerline miles maintained per 1,000 population
- Percentage of streets rated 85 percent or better on standard rating system
- Cost per centerline mile repaved by contractors (in thousands of dollars)
- Total cost per ton of materials applied—city crews and contractors

Source: North Carolina Local Government Performance Measurement Project (1997).

Illustrative Outcome Indicators Included in Vermont's Agency of Human Services Community Profiles

Pregnant Women and Newborns Thrive
- Percentage of pregnant women receiving early prenatal care (entry in first trimester)
- Percentage of low-birth-weight babies (under 5.5 pounds)
- Percentage of births where families receive "new baby" visits

Infants and Children Thrive
- Infant mortality rate
- Rate of injuries (ages 0 to 9) resulting in hospitalization
- Child mortality rate (deaths from all causes; ages 1 to 14)

Children Are Ready for School
- Rate of full immunization at kindergarten entry

Children Succeed in School
- Percentage of children meeting standard on developmental reading assessment at 2nd grade
- Percentage of students receiving special education services
- Average SAT scores (verbal, math)
- Percentage of high school dropouts

Children Live in Stable, Supported Families
- Percentage of children in poverty
- Percentage of children in families receiving food stamps (proxy for child poverty)
- Rate of out-of-home placements (for children under 18 years old)

Youth Choose Healthy Behaviors
- Rate of teen sexually transmitted diseases
- Young teen pregnancy rate (15- to 17-year-olds)
- Rate of youth in custody for delinquency
- Teen violent death rate (homicide, suicide, injuries)

Source: Murphey (1999).

Final Thoughts

There are many things to consider in establishing the scope of a CPM. Two key points to keep in mind are:

- It is better to have a few meaningful indicators than multiple poor ones.
- It is preferable to concentrate on outcome indicators, rather than resorting to easy-to-develop workload or input indicators.

Note

1. For more detailed information on performance indicators, see Hatry (1999).

Preparing for Data Collection: How to Define Indicators in Measurable Terms

It is critical to develop and provide clear and thorough definitions of each data element used in a CPM effort.

Once performance indicators have been selected in any interagency CPM effort, it is important to convert them into terms that enable collection of data that are as comparable as possible. If jurisdictions or agencies participating in a cooperative (voluntary) CPM do not believe the data collected are comparable, they will be reluctant to use the data and may even drop out of the effort. Similarly, external efforts should also attempt to obtain comparable data in order to promote the usefulness and acceptance of their data. However, *although comparability of data is very important, data collected from multiple governments for any performance indicator will inevitably reflect at least small differences in how the data were collected—regardless of the effort made to avoid such differences. Variations occur because some jurisdictions or agencies may use somewhat different definitions, data collection procedures, or aggregation methods. CPM participants and users of CPM reports need to be aware that the data obtained through these efforts will invariably be* roughly *or* approximately *comparable—not absolutely comparable. However, it is more preferable to have data that are "roughly right" than to be "precisely ignorant."*

This chapter discusses the initial steps required before actual data collection can begin:

1. Convert performance indicators into *clearly defined* data elements.
2. Adjust indicators for size differences, where necessary.
3. Convert explanatory factors into *clearly defined* data elements.

These steps help to establish definitions and procedures that are likely to be acceptable and feasible for regular (such as annual) data collection by most, if not all, agencies included in a CPM effort. Even in cases where CPM is not conducted annually (such as some external or ad hoc efforts), most of these steps are needed or desirable.

Step One: Convert Each Performance Indicator into Clearly Defined Data Elements

Before data can be collected from multiple agencies, the data elements needed to calculate each indicator must be clearly identified and defined. This enables personnel to seek comparable data across agencies. Data elements are the separate pieces of data that must be obtained from each agency (or existing data source) in order to calculate the value of an indicator. Relatively few indicators are obtained from a single "number." Many have at least a numerator and denominator—e.g., indicators adjusted to account for variations in the size of the population served (see step 2).

In cases where indicators are relatively straightforward, the name of the indicator may identify the data elements involved, such as the "number of violent crimes per 1,000 population." Yet in such cases, definitions of terms (such as a definition of a violent crime) are needed to ensure that all agencies provide comparable data.

Familiarity with the ways agencies obtain and record data is highly desirable for this step. (This is a key reason for involving representatives of agencies covered by the CPM.) CPM staff need to clearly specify how each indicator is defined and calculated, identifying the data elements for both the numerator and denominator, where applicable.

Developing data elements is facilitated when common definitions of particular terms already exist. Such definitions may have been developed because of requirements for reporting to the federal government or to professional organizations that collect and report data. For example, common definitions of major categories of crime—such as violent crime and property crime (which, combined, are reported as "Part 1 crimes")—have been developed for national reporting to the FBI. The FBI then publishes crime data provided by local police agencies in its annual *Uniform Crime Report* (UCR). Several indicators for police, fire, and library services used by the ICMA Consortium involve such commonly defined terms, as do some police indicators used by North Carolina's CPM effort. In such cases, data collection instruments can reference the common definition. Although common definitions such as these are helpful, they do not resolve all differences in data collection and reporting. For example, controversy remains as to the way in which police officers classify specific incidents and the extent to which crimes are reported in each jurisdiction.

Common definitions are not available for all indicators, even in cases where a phrase is commonly used to describe an activity or service. An example from police indicators selected by the ICMA Consortium illustrates this point. "Average response time to *top priority* calls from dispatch to arrival" was selected as one of the indicators of deterrence/patrol services by the ICMA police technical advisory committee (TAC). The initial rounds of data collection by Consortium members revealed wide ranges of data for this indicator. When data were checked, it became clear that jurisdictions were not including the same types of calls in their data. To promote greater comparability, the definition of top priority calls provided on the data collection template was clarified to read: "A top priority call requires an immediate police response. A top priority call includes immediate threat to life, violent criminal act in progress, suspect pursuing citizen, imminent critical danger, or the possibility of major property loss."

Similarly, it became clear that one of the road maintenance descriptive indicators—number of lane miles maintained—was being interpreted in more than one way. Some jurisdictions reported the number of miles for which they had maintenance responsibility; others reported the number of miles actually worked on during the reporting period. The definition for this indicator was changed to read: "Count lane miles of road for which the jurisdiction is responsible regardless of whether they are worked on."

Including agency representatives in developing data elements enables identification of indicators that are commonly defined and measured because, in some cases, there may be considerable discrepancy in how participants measure or collect data for an indicator. For example, discussion in the ICMA Consortium's neighborhood services TAC revealed that several potential parks indicators (such as "attendance at parks and recreation areas" and "number of accidents, injuries, or crimes at parks and recreation areas") were not uniformly measured. These were subsequently eliminated.

What can be done when agencies use different definitions? Some options are:

- Delete the indicator if differences in how it is defined vary too widely among agencies.
- Exclude from the comparison those agencies whose definitions are significantly different from others.
- Include those agencies—but with annotations explaining the different definitions.
- If several agencies use one definition and others use another, show both groups in separate tables and charts, clearly identifying the different performance indicators.

Although availability of uniform data among participating agencies is important, it should not always be the dominant factor in selecting indicators. A desirable indicator can be selected even if some agencies are unable to report on it initially—either because their definitions vary considerably from those of the other agencies, or they do not collect the needed data. Over time, such agencies may be able to modify their definitions or data collection practices, enabling them to submit the data in the same form as the other agencies. In some cases, agencies may not be able to report on specific indicators because they are not responsible for providing the corresponding service.

It is critical *to develop and provide clear and thorough definitions of each data element used in a CPM effort*. If the effort involves direct data collection from agencies, definitions may be organized as a "data dictionary" for participating agencies. The dictionary should thoroughly describe and define each data element (perhaps with examples), with descriptions reviewed and updated annually as necessary. The set of definitions should be dated and provided to agency personnel *each year* that the comparisons are made, ensuring that new agency staff have a copy—and the most recent one. Participants in working groups or advisory committees for voluntary or mandatory efforts should also receive dictionaries.

In CPM efforts that do not involve *direct* submission of data from agencies, those responsible for the comparative data also need to define indicators in terms of data elements to ensure comparable data from different agencies. This applies to external (such as media- or other third-party-initiated) or internal efforts where an agency is comparing its own data with available data from similar agencies. The staff of such efforts should check with the participating agencies to determine whether the data used are based on the same elements and definitions. Resulting reports need to clearly specify the indicator definitions and the data elements used for each.

Common Problems in Data Definition

Each data element in each indicator must be clearly defined. When identifying different age or income groups, for example, general terms such as "juveniles," "adults," "elderly" or "low income" are not sufficiently specific. Age groups should be defined preferably in terms of specific ages (e.g., under 18 years of age, over 65 years of age). Income-related explanatory factors should specify the income level to be used or other accepted proxy measures for the group of interest. An example of the latter might be the number of students eligible for free or reduced-cost lunch programs.

Indicators involving time periods, such as average response times, present a special problem. The data element definition should specify the start and stop times for the time period and the way in which time is to be reported (e.g., minutes, hours, days, calendar days, workdays, etc.). In some cases, indicators may include more than one time period to reflect different stages in the process leading to particular outcomes. Following are examples of indicators that involve time periods and how such time periods may be specified:

- Average number of calendar days from the time a dangerous building code violation is *first reported* until the inspector's *first inspection*, for cases initiated during the reporting period.
- Average time from the *receipt* of a top priority police telephone call to *dispatch*.
- Average time from *dispatch* to *arrival* (of emergency vehicle).

Identifying data elements for indicators that use staff data also requires care. While the indicator "number of employees" seems straightforward, there may be different categories of employees (such as civilian and uniformed, or "sworn," personnel in police or fire departments). In such cases, certain types of employees may be more appropriately included in efficiency indicators or as explanatory factors for some outcomes than others.

Definitions involving "number of employees" need to specify how employees are to be counted, since some employees may work part-time, while others work full-time. This can be particularly important for certain employees, such as police and fire personnel. Employee data submitted in terms of "full-time equivalent employees" (FTE) is preferable since this method adjusts for differences in the use of part-time employees and overtime. Some organizations may have difficulty making this conversion, however. An alternative approach (used by the ICMA Consortium) is to ask agencies to report the total number of *paid* employee hours. This number is the product of some specific number of weeks and hours used to define "FTE" (e.g., 52 weeks × 40 hours per week = 2,080).

A CPM is also likely to run into data *timing* and *timeliness* problems. It is important to establish the time period for the comparative data. Most CPM efforts collect and report data for one year. But which year? For example, should data be reported in terms of the calendar year or the fiscal year (if different)? Fiscal years vary among jurisdictions and agencies, and while many organizations share a common fiscal year (such as July 1–June 30, or January 1–December 31), differences invariably occur. However, many agencies prefer fiscal year reporting because their expenditure data are calculated on that basis. Such data are then used to calculate efficiency indicators based on expenditures and staff. Expenditures are also sometimes used as explanatory factors.

Timeliness is vital for usefulness. Schedules for data collection and reporting should allow for data collection shortly after the end of the selected reporting period. This enables the early reporting of data to agencies included in the CPM (once checking and data analysis are complete)—while the data are still timely. Although annual data collection is appropriate for CPM reporting purposes, more frequent collection (e.g., quarterly) is more useful for most agencies and jurisdictions.

Step Two: Adjust Indicators to Reflect Size Differences, Where Necessary

A key characteristic of interjurisdictional comparative performance measurement is that it involves data from multiple agencies. Because of this, adjustments must be made for size differences among agencies or jurisdictions—sometimes called "normalizing." It would not be appropriate, for example, to simply use the quantity of a particular outcome when comparing jurisdictions of vastly different size, such as Los Angeles, California, and Richmond, Virginia. Agencies serving large populations will invariably have much larger "raw numbers" for such indicators.

To address size variations in CPM efforts, indicators need to be adjusted ("normalized") for population size. This is typically done by dividing an indicator by the relevant population associated with that service. Some forms of normalization are familiar because certain types of data are commonly reported in normalized terms, such as crimes per 1,000 population, the infant mortality rate, and graduation rates (or, conversely, school dropout rates). Other kinds of data, such as input or resource data, also are commonly normalized. Terms

Attention to data collection pays dividends in terms of the acceptance and usefulness of the effort.

Collecting Data for Comparison

Once indicators have been converted into data elements and defined in measurable terms, data collection can begin. In cooperative and external CPM efforts for which agencies directly provide data to the analysts, the collection stage encompasses several steps:

1. Develop data collection instruments and procedures.
2. Identify the sources of data.
3. Collect data.
4. Check and correct data (data quality control).
5. Revise procedures as needed.

External efforts that do *not* collect data directly from agencies covered by the CPM also need to address most of these steps. The key difference in such efforts is that the steps generally will not directly involve the agencies.

Step One: Develop Data Collection Instruments and Procedures

A key step in CPM is determining that similar, compatible data collection procedures are used by the agencies or jurisdictions being compared. For efforts in which the agencies have agreed to participate and provide data for the comparison, analysts must first identify data collection instruments and procedures. As noted previously, definitions of each data element used in a CPM should be compiled into a "data dictionary." This document will provide guidance to agency personnel and CPM staff. Agency personnel need this information in advance of data submission, however, so they can collect data in a way that enables them to report the data as specified.

One decision facing a CPM effort is whether data collection instruments will be paper or electronic. Data collection will likely involve paper forms (templates) initially. Computerized data collection might then occur after the first year or two of the effort. The ICMA Consortium developed an electronic data collection program after the initial round of collection was performed with paper templates. This was done, in part, to reduce problems resulting from data entry and computational errors on the part of participating jurisdictions. In electronic data collection, agencies provide raw data for various data elements and computers automatically calculate many indicators directly from these data. This procedure avoids human errors that inevitably occur when calculations are performed by participating agencies.

In cases where data are electronically transmitted, the software program should include as many computer-generated checks on the data as possible. For example, a plausible range could be identified for every data element. If an agency entered a number outside that range, the computer would send a "Please check: Out of plausible range" message. A similar feature could be developed to "flag" significant changes in values from one year to the next. It may not be feasible to begin automatic data checking until at least one year of data collection is complete (to enable identification of plausible ranges, for example), but this process could save considerable time and effort.

Developing the data collection template is a major task, and the details of this process are beyond the scope of this report. However, the key goal of this step is to convert the definitions developed for each data element into clearly understandable, specific instructions to ensure that staff of different agencies will provide the same kind of data. The template needs to specify clearly how the data are to be reported and provide definitions and formulas for calculating indicators, where applicable. This is desirable even in cases where data are entered electronically. This process enables agency personnel to readily explain their calculations to others locally and, if they desire, check the electronic calculations.

Step Two: Identify the Sources of Data

External CPM efforts that do not receive data directly from involved agencies must identify existing, accessible sources of needed data. These sources generally include reports or records from federal and state agencies or national organizations, including professional organizations. Data from these sources often are based on information obtained from service-providing agencies themselves. The Annie E. Casey Foundation's annual *Kids Count Data Book* is one example of an external CPM that primarily uses data from U.S. government agencies.

In cooperative and external CPM efforts where agencies provide data directly to the effort, most indicator data come from the records of those agencies. Some agencies may have to make adjustments to some of their current data collection procedures in order to provide data as specified for some indicators. For example, some agencies may need to begin collecting data on response times for various services or collect data for "start" and "stop" times differently from previous methods. Such modifications will require some time and effort. Once the process has been established, maintaining it over time should be relatively simple and inexpensive.

Some data may need to be obtained from records of entities other than those participating in the effort, such as demographic data from the U.S. Census or employment data compiled by the Bureau of Labor Statistics. Such data are likely to be used primarily in explanatory factors or to adjust indicators for size differences among agencies (see chapter 4). While data from such outside sources are uniformly collected, they are often out-of-date. As a result, some CPM efforts might, for example, use 1999 outcome data in the numerator of an indicator, but 1990 population data in the denominator. The U.S. Census Bureau provides updated, selected population estimates for states and some local governments, but not in sufficient detail for some comparisons. CPM managers might arrange with one of the commercial firms making credible, regular, detailed estimates of demographic data to update census data. While such data may be far from perfect, they are better than 10-year-old census data and, in addition, the estimates are calculated in a consistent manner across agencies. The latter would not be the case if each agency in the CPM effort provided its own updated estimates using a variety of procedures.

For most indicators, records kept by each jurisdiction or agency are likely to be the primary source of that organization's information. However, for some indicators, new forms of, and procedures for, data collection may be required. The two procedures most commonly used are customer surveys and trained observer ratings. It is beyond the scope of this report to discuss in detail how to collect these types of data. However, an overview of each is provided below. (Sources for more detailed information on these topics are identified in the reference section.)

Customer Surveys

Surveys of customers have begun to be perceived nationally, if not internationally, as a major source of evaluation feedback for public services and as an important component of public accountability. Use of this procedure is growing significantly at all levels of government as well as in the private, nonprofit sector.

Surveys of various stakeholder groups are a key mechanism for obtaining data on citizen or customer satisfaction and service quality characteristics, such as the perceived timeliness of service delivery or courtesy of the personnel providing services. Surveys can also provide key information about customer behavior resulting from certain services (such as obtaining a job after participation in a job training program). Such surveys should appeal to an agency that wants to be, and be perceived as, customer focused. In addition, surveys can and should seek from respondents specific information about service problems and suggestions for service improvement. While this information may not be used for CPM purposes, it is highly valuable to participating agencies.

Although many jurisdictions and agencies regularly survey their citizens or customers, this practice will likely be new to some participants in a CPM effort.

Agencies may be concerned about including indicators based on survey data, since this procedure is potentially expensive and time consuming. However, one survey can provide data for many performance indicators. This is the case both for citizen surveys covering a variety of services (and multiple agencies) and for surveys of a single agency's customers.

To obtain similar data for indicators based on surveys, it is desirable that each agency use a common survey (questionnaire). For example, the ICMA Consortium developed a common customer survey for participating jurisdictions. The questionnaire was developed to promote comparability of data by ensuring jurisdictions' survey questions had common wording and response choices. This survey includes questions about various aspects of police and neighborhood services. The steering committee asks each jurisdiction to administer the instrument to its citizens or to include some or all of the questions in the jurisdiction's own citizen survey (where applicable). Data have been accepted from jurisdictions whose own customer survey questions and response categories are quite similar to those developed for the Consortium. Due to the added cost of conducting surveys, not all jurisdictions have undertaken them.

Customers are not always citizens. Other agencies or organizations can be the customers of agencies that provide support services, such as vehicle or building maintenance. The ICMA Consortium also developed a survey for customers of internal support services.

Participating agencies will likely need guidance regarding survey administration to ensure they use reasonably similar methods of obtaining survey data. Guidance is particularly important for the more technical aspects of survey administration, such as selecting a "sample" of the desired survey population, determining the appropriate sample size, obtaining adequate response rates, and tabulating responses. Participants also may need information about administering questionnaires—either by mail, telephone, or in person (at home or at a public facility, such as a library or park), or a combination of these—and appropriate procedures for each. CPM participants should also be advised that it may be appropriate to use a consultant or seek assistance from a local university regarding the more technical aspects of the survey.[1]

Trained Observer Ratings

Although not designed specifically for CPM purposes, trained observer ratings enable comparison of indicators that cannot be obtained from agency records. These ratings can be used to generate data for indicators of conditions that can be seen by an observer or measured by other physical senses. Typical examples of such indicators include the cleanliness of streets, parks, or other public facilities; the condition of public facilities; the smoothness of streets and roads; the adequacy of light provided by streetlights; and the condition and visibility of traffic signs. Some trained observer rating techniques employ some form of technology to measure conditions, such as "roughometers" that measure road smoothness. Indicators based on trained observer ratings are usually reported as percentages, such as "percentage of streets rated as clean."

Trained observer rating procedures generally use photographic or written guidelines to enable different observers to produce comparable ratings of actual conditions. Photographic guidelines generally include several photographs showing variations in conditions (such as different levels of street cleanliness). Each photograph depicts a different rating value (such as "clean," "moderately littered," or "heavily littered"). Observers may be citizen volunteers, college students, or government agency personnel, among others. After training in use of the guidelines, observers are sent to selected locations to rate actual conditions according to the scales.[2] As with customer surveys, each covered agency should use a similar trained observer rating procedure so that its data are useful for the CPM effort.

Step Three: Collect Data

Data collection varies by type of CPM. For most external efforts, such as those performed by the media (newspapers, magazines, or journals) or advocacy groups, analysts primarily collect data from existing sources. These sources might include agency records that are published or publicly accessible, or reports compiled by state or federal agencies. These efforts include two key data collection activities: (1) accessing the data and recording them on the instrument or form the CPM is using (if any) and (2) performing calculations needed to convert the data into the desired data elements. (Checking data for accuracy is discussed in step 4.)

For efforts in which agencies compile and submit their own data for analysis (cooperative and some external CPMs), data collection involves several steps. Agency personnel must extract data from the appropriate agency records (or other sources, such as census data), perform the appropriate calculations (where needed), enter data on the data collection instrument, check the data entered for accuracy, and submit the instruments to CPM personnel.

Agencies directly submitting data for CPM efforts may need technical assistance during the data collection process regarding how to calculate specific data elements, what agency records data to use for a particular element, and the use of surveys or trained observer ratings. The ICMA Consortium addressed the technical assistance needs of jurisdictions by establishing a training program for new Consortium members. This program promotes an understanding of performance measurement and helps jurisdictions understand the Consortium's data collection instrument and find appropriate sources of data within their own records. Although initial training is highly desirable, it is probably not sufficient, particularly since staff turnover makes it unlikely that the personnel originally trained will remain in their positions over the long run. Periodic "refresher" training for participating agencies is likely to be needed.

CPM analysts also need to send periodic "quality reminders" to agencies that submit CPM data. These reminders can address common data reporting problems and how to avoid them. They can also be used to "spread the word" when new data problems arise (such as interpretation questions). Once CPM personnel have resolved a specific issue, information describing the problem and how it should be handled can be transmitted to all participating agencies.

One method of data collection, notwithstanding its added accuracy problems, is commonly used in ad hoc CPM efforts conducted by agencies and sometimes by journalists. This approach involves agency personnel making telephone calls to similar agencies (or journalists to the agencies of interest) in order to obtain data on specific indicators or data elements. This is not the ideal way to obtain data because of the considerable likelihood of reporting and transcription errors. In addition, there is little opportunity to exercise quality control steps in these circumstances or to ascertain that the data reported were obtained or calculated in comparable ways.

Step Four: Check and Correct Data

Checking data for accuracy and correcting erroneous data (sometimes referred to as "data cleaning") are very important steps for CPM efforts. Accurate data contribute to valid comparisons. Unfortunately, inaccuracy can be introduced into data in many ways. In order to appear more successful, some agencies may deliberately manipulate their data or adopt other dysfunctional practices, such as selecting clients with fewer problems.[3] While it is difficult to detect deliberate misreporting of data without auditing agency records (a more costly step than most CPM efforts are likely to undertake), less-costly quality control steps should enable identification of many, if not most, data errors.

This section provides suggestions for data-checking practices, primarily derived from experiences of the ICMA Consortium. The suggestions immediately following apply to cooperative and external CPM efforts for which agencies directly submit data. Quality control for other CPM efforts is discussed later in this section.

- Data checking should take place at several points in the data collection and analysis process. As noted previously, data checking should be part of any program for electronically transmitted data. The staff of the CPM effort and the agencies submitting data should share responsibility for checking data.
- Before agencies submit their data, personnel responsible for data entry should check and double-check the data. Some spot-checking is desirable, including recalculation and reversion to the original form (such as agency records or computerized data) to confirm the accuracy of the data entered. The most current year's data should be compared against data submitted in the previous year (if applicable)—this helps identify changes in data collection practices between the years.

First Round

The data need to be checked for the following types of errors:

- *Extremely high/low values.* Extreme values, or "outliers," are easier to locate at the time the data are compared with that of other agencies. However, personnel familiar with the service area likely can identify unusual values. Outliers may result from incorrect definitions for a particular data element, a typographical error, or some special circumstance that requires explanatory information.
- *Inconsistencies.* For example, an agency might indicate that particular data are not available, but later report an indicator based on that kind of data.
- *Missing/incorrectly entered data.* The analyst should check for missing data and verify that data were entered in the appropriate format (such as percentages rather than whole numbers).
- *Comments.* If agencies enter comments on the data collection form, review of such comments may identify possible errors. For example, these comments may indicate that agency personnel did not understand the nature of the data requested, used an inappropriate technique to calculate a particular data item, or provided partial rather than complete data.

In cooperative CPM efforts, agency or jurisdiction representatives to the effort also need to review their data prior to submission. This step underscores the importance the agency places on the effort. For mandatory efforts, agency or jurisdiction officials responsible for the data should review the information prior to submission.

Second Round

CPM personnel may initially review data submitted by each individual agency. Following that, data from the set of participating agencies might be compared. Developing spreadsheets facilitates such comparison by arraying the data in each category from all participants. Things to look for at this stage include:

- *Extremely high/low values.* Values that may not appear extreme when reviewed in isolation may appear extreme when compared with other agencies.
- *Computer errors.* Where calculations are performed electronically, some random spot-checking of the accuracy of those calculations is desirable. This is particularly important when any programming changes have been made—including changes as simple as renumbering indicators to adjust for additions or deletions. Similarly, spot-checking ensures that computer-calculated values are entered only when *all* of the data needed for a given calculation are present.
- *Similarity to other publicly reported data.* In some cases, documents are available that report on indicators the same as or similar to those collected for a CPM effort. One example of this is police crime data published in the FBI's *Uniform Crime Reports*. In such cases, it is desirable to compare the data submitted for the CPM effort with the reported data (even if they are not from identical time periods). Large discrepancies between the CPM data and the other data should be explored as potential errors.

CPM staff should contact, in writing, any agency for which potential discrepancies have been identified. Care should be taken to clearly identify the problem indicators. In cases where the suspect indicator is derived from multiple data elements—such as a numerator and denominator—all data used to derive it should also be clearly identified. The agency should be asked to check its data and provide corrected data, or confirm the accuracy of the original data.

CPM efforts need to establish "decision rules" governing the exclusion of data from CPM reports in cases where staff believe data to be incorrect, but cannot verify that with the agency in question. Experiences of the ICMA Consortium indicate that on a few occasions, jurisdictions have not been responsive to requests for data checking. In addition, jurisdictions have, in some cases, verified data as correct, but later discovered they were incorrect. Such verification of inaccurate data may occur because of problems with an agency's data collection procedures. For example, data for certain police indicators reported by one jurisdiction in the early stages of the ICMA Consortium showed poor performance in crime clearance relative to other jurisdictions. This situation came to the attention of the city council, which asked for an explanation. Further exploration by police officials revealed procedural problems with the reporting of case statistics by field officers and programming problems with the department's database. This city was able to resolve both issues, which were unknown to department officials until data checking brought them to light.

Decisions about rules for the exclusion of data under certain conditions should be made with representatives of the agencies included in the CPM. These rules then need to be conveyed to the agencies so they are aware that their data may be excluded under certain conditions. Care should be taken, however, to avoid excluding data unnecessarily. Not all data that appear to be unusual are incorrect. For example, several jurisdictions in the ICMA Consortium demonstrated large differences from one reporting year to the next in data reported for "operating and maintenance expenditures per paved lane mile maintained." While checking revealed valid data, there were a variety of reasons for the expenditure shifts, including deferred maintenance policies, unusual weather, and natural disasters. In such cases, explanatory notes should be included to explain such circumstances (see chapter 7).

Final Round

A final round of data checking needs to be done before the CPM report is completed. To facilitate checking, data might be arrayed in tables or graphs (such as bar charts; see chapter 6). Displaying data in this way usually makes some potential errors more noticeable. For example, values that might not have appeared to be extreme on a spreadsheet may appear visually extreme in a bar chart.

Draft copies of the report should be distributed to participating agencies for one last data checking before a final version is prepared. CPM analysts should flag data that appear suspect, as well as any data that were previously questioned but not yet corrected or confirmed by the agency.

In cases where comparisons involve percentage changes from prior years' data, CPM analysts should check agencies with unusually large changes. Such variations may be due to errors or changes in data collection procedures over time. While there is no exact rule for identifying an unusually large change, in general, shifts of 25 percent or more should be examined. The size of indicator values needs to be considered, however, when applying such guidelines. If the values reported are very small, a modest raise in indicator value (e.g., from 1 to 2) results in a large percentage increase (in this case, 100 percent). Yet valid explanations may exist for substantial differences in indicators from year to year, as in the road maintenance example discussed above.

In cases where customer surveys provide indicator data for CPM efforts, analysts should review the questionnaires in order to verify the comparability of question and response categories. Similarly, survey methodology should also be examined, confirming that reasonably acceptable survey procedures were used to collect the data. Data from surveys based on nonscientific procedures, such as questionnaires left in offices or libraries, or printed in newspapers, should probably be excluded from CPM efforts. Analysts should also determine whether reasonable response rates were obtained. (Surveys with response rates below approximately 40 percent should be excluded, or at least be identified as having low response rates).

For external CPM efforts that rely on available data rather than data submitted directly to the effort by covered agencies, some of the quality control steps listed above can still be applied. For example, CPM analysts should check data for extremely high or low values, since even published reports can include data errors. Comparisons with other publicly reported data may be feasible in some cases. Analysts might also look for changes that might affect comparisons across time periods, such as changes in the definitions of data elements or in agency data-reporting practices. In addition, calculations performed by CPM analysts need to be checked for computer or human error.

It is not necessary for all compared agencies to use the same data collection procedures—whether the data are obtained from trained observers, customer surveys, or agency records. However, the analysts need to ascertain that the procedures used by different agencies provide reasonably similar information. Analysts can interview agency personnel (in person or over the telephone) to determine if this is the case.

Step Five: Revise Procedures As Needed

For CPM efforts involving repeated (such as annual) rounds of data collection, definitions, data collection instruments, and procedures need to be reviewed and revised, based on the experiences of the initial and succeeding rounds. Agency representatives who were involved in working groups or advisory committees during the identification of indicators and data elements should be included in this process if possible. It is highly unlikely that the initial efforts to define indicators and develop data collection instruments will be without errors. Numerous "glitches" will undoubtedly be discovered when the initial data are submitted, and modifications to data elements or procedures will be required to address them. The ICMA Consortium working groups, for example, continued refining indicators and revising definitions throughout the first three rounds of annual data collection.

One concern associated with revising data definitions is, What happens to comparability of data over time? Analysts should determine whether the change in a definition or indicator is so substantial that it is inappropriate to compare data from different time periods, or whether it is a sufficiently minor change that such comparisons are appropriate. In the latter case, CPM reports should make clear that even though percentage change data are provided, a change in definition occurred that may have an effect on the data reported for different time periods.

For ongoing CPM efforts involving special data collection, analysts need to regularly review performance indicators with the participating agencies. An annual meeting of CPM working groups might involve discussion as to whether modifications to any indicators or data element definitions are needed for increased data comparability. This review also might consider whether the collection of indicators for which few agencies are able to provide data should continue. CPM staff could generate lists of elements for which limited data have been provided for two or three data collection cycles and consider these as candidates for exclusion in subsequent data collection. Care should be taken, however, that key outcomes are not included in this group.

At each review, analysts should also consider improving or adding outcome indicators, particularly for those services that had relatively few indicators in the first place. It may be useful to designate a subcommittee for this purpose. A good example of updating indicators is the Vermont Agency of Human Services' Community Profiles effort, which has continued to refine and add indicators since its first report in 1995. Its 1998 report had several additions, including a new outcome category, "elders and people with disabilities live with dignity and independence in settings they prefer," and several indicators associated with this category. Several indicators of youth "developmental assets" (strengths) were added in 1998, using data based on responses to a student survey in Vermont school districts.

Data collection deserves considerable attention in all CPM efforts. As the old saying goes, "Garbage in, garbage out." Unless efforts are made to ensure that data are as accurate and comparable as possible, both the credibility and fairness of the effort are likely to be in question. Attention to data collection pays dividends in terms of the acceptance and usefulness of the effort.

Notes

1. For more information on constructing customer surveys, see Hatry et al. (1998), Fink and Kosecoff (1998), and Rubin and Babbie (1997): chapter 7, "Constructing Outcome Measurement Instruments," and chapter 8, "The Logic of Sampling."
2. For more information on trained observer ratings, see Greiner (1994).
3. For a discussion of functional and dysfunctional organization responses to CPM, see Gormley and Weimer (1999).

Chapter 6

One of CPM's major purposes is to stimulate agencies to make improvements. Providing information on why some agencies are achieving better results than others can help accomplish this.

Analyzing Comparative Performance Information

This chapter describes options for analyzing the data collected through CPM efforts. These options are grouped by two questions:

- How well is the agency doing on the performance indicators?
- Why did the agency perform that way?

How Well Is the Agency Doing?

The following options suggest how to examine an agency's level of performance relative to other agencies. All or some of these options might be used.

1. *Present the data without any further analysis.* The values for each agency's indicators can be presented without ranking or rating them in any way. This process applies mostly to indicators that are not performance indicators, such as expenditures for particular services, and the agencies and their indicator values might simply be presented alphabetically. For example, the U.S. Census Bureau reports on state and local government expenditures for each service area without additional analysis, and a recent Urban Institute paper, *State Child Welfare Spending at a Glance* (Waters Boots 1999), provides a variety of expenditure data for each state, with the states listed in alphabetical order. Such reports are intended primarily to present data, not to provide any evaluative information. For performance information, however, the basic data will usually be much more useful if more is actually done with the information (described below).

2. *Calculate and provide information on the average (mean) and/or the median of all the agencies being examined, and the standard deviation.* The arithmetic average of all

agencies is frequently used in comparisons so that each agency can compare itself with this average. The drawback to averages, however, is that large outlier values can substantially alter (and distort) the average. Presenting the median (the middle value), therefore, is often an attractive option. (For an even number of agencies, the median is calculated by averaging the two middle values.) For further clarification, both the mean and median might be presented (see exhibit 6-1, where the mean is based on national data, and exhibit 6-2). The standard deviation shows how the values are distributed.

3. *Rank the agencies on each indicator.* This is a very popular approach, and it is simple to do. Those preparing the report have only to array the agencies by their values on each indicator. Thus, if there are 100 agencies in the analysis, they will be ranked from 1 to 100. (Agencies with the same values on a particular indicator are generally given a ranking range. For example, if the third, fourth, and fifth agencies all have the same values, each is given the same rank—"3–5".) Note that for some performance indicators, such as response times, lower values indicate better performance.

Ranking agencies means that there will always be a first and a last place finisher. Unfortunately, this can lead to unfair judgments about the performance of some agencies. For example, if all (or many) of the jurisdictions' values on a given indicator are similar and the differences among them are not important, the ranking will present a misleading picture. Similarly, if all the agencies are actually performing quite well on any reasonable interpretation of the data, they will still be ranked 1 to 100. If all the agencies are performing poorly on the indicator, there will still be performers that appear to be doing well—those at the top of the rankings.

Some users of this type of information believe this situation is acceptable because it serves to motivate those agencies at the bottom of the heap and provides recognition to the top agencies—even though their performance may still be poor or not much higher than those with lower rankings. On the whole, presenting ranking as the only analysis often will not provide a fair picture.

4. *Develop a rating system for each indicator; assign a "grade" to each jurisdiction.* This option is represented by the increasingly popular "score card" or "report card" format, which assigns grades, such as A, B, C, D, and (sometimes) F. (This is analogous to the ratings by movie critics giving perhaps one, two, three, or four stars to a motion picture.) The recent 50-state report card published in *Governing* magazine used this approach (Barrett and Greene 1999). Each state was given a grade from A through D on each of its state management systems, including financial, capital, human resources, managing for results, and information technology management.

Developing a rating system, however, requires special effort, particularly in the selection of rating criteria. Sometimes rating decisions are primarily judgmental, such as those used in the *Governing* example above. However, there are many ways to establish the grades, including the following:

- Use "experts" to select reasonable boundary values.
- Use past values to select the quartiles (if four grades are to be used), quintiles (if five grades are to be used), and so on that represent the boundaries between grades.

EXHIBIT 6-1

Example of Data Analysis Showing Comparison with the National Average

Rhode Island RI

National Composite Rank [18]

Indicators	Percent Change 1985 to 1995		Trend Data 1985	Trend Data 1995	National Rank *National Rank is based on 1995 figures*
Percent low birth-weight babies 1985-1995	STATE	8	6.3	6.8	[19]
	NATIONAL		6.8	7.3	
Infant mortality rate (deaths per 1,000 live births) 1985-1995	STATE	12	8.2	7.2	[19]
	NATIONAL		10.6	7.6	
Child death rate (deaths per 100,000 children ages 1-14) 1985-1995	STATE	17	24	20	[2]
	NATIONAL		34	28	
Rate of teen deaths by accident, homicide, and suicide (deaths per 100,000 teens ages 15-19) 1985-1995	STATE	15	39	33	[2]
	NATIONAL		63	65	
Teen birth rate (births per 1,000 females ages 15-17) 1985-1995	STATE	29	21	27	[16]
	NATIONAL		31	36	
Juvenile violent crime arrest rate (arrests per 100,000 youths ages 10-17) 1985-1995	STATE	62	301	489	[36]
	NATIONAL		305	507	
Percent of teens who are high school dropouts (ages 16-19) 1985-1995	STATE	33	15	10	[31]
	NATIONAL		11	10	
Percent of teens not attending school and not working (ages 16-19) 1985-1995	STATE	20	10	8	[18]
	NATIONAL		11	9	
Percent of children in poverty 1985-1995	STATE	6	18	17	[24]
	NATIONAL		21	21	
Percent of families with children headed by a single parent 1985-1995	STATE	27	22	28	[40]
	NATIONAL		22	26	

WORSE — ZERO — BETTER

▨ Patterned bars indicate national change. ▪ Solid bars indicate state change.

Source: Annie E. Casey Foundation (1998). *Kids Count Data Book*, p. 119. Used by permission.

EXHIBIT 6-2

Example of Data Analysis Showing the Mean, Median, and Standard Deviation

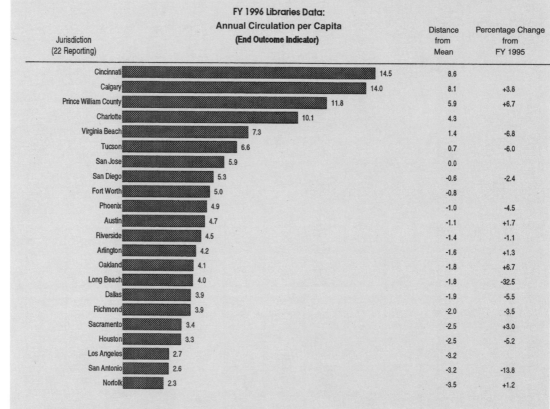

FY 1996 Libraries Data:
Annual Circulation per Capita
(End Outcome Indicator)

Jurisdiction (22 Reporting)	Annual Circulation per Capita	Distance from Mean	Percentage Change from FY 1995
Cincinnati	14.5	8.6	
Calgary	14.0	8.1	+3.8
Prince William County	11.8	5.9	+6.7
Charlotte	10.1	4.3	
Virginia Beach	7.3	1.4	-6.8
Tucson	6.6	0.7	-6.0
San Jose	5.9	0.0	
San Diego	5.3	-0.6	-2.4
Fort Worth	5.0	-0.8	
Phoenix	4.9	-1.0	-4.5
Austin	4.7	-1.1	+1.7
Riverside	4.5	-1.4	-1.1
Arlington	4.2	-1.6	+1.3
Oakland	4.1	-1.8	+6.7
Long Beach	4.0	-1.8	-32.5
Dallas	3.9	-1.9	-5.5
Richmond	3.9	-2.0	-3.5
Sacramento	3.4	-2.5	+3.0
Houston	3.3	-2.5	-5.2
Los Angeles	2.7	-3.2	
San Antonio	2.6	-3.2	-13.8
Norfolk	2.3	-3.5	+1.2

Note: The mean is 5.9; the median is 4.6; and the standard deviation is 3.5.

Circulation includes all materials of any format (e.g., written and audio-visual materials), including renewals that are checked out for use outside the library. Circulation per capita includes combined circulation reported by jurisdictions from central libraries, branches, and bookmobiles.

Some of the variation in circulation rates among jurisdictions may be due to differences in factors such as the availability of branch libraries, the overall number of facilities, number of hours open, size and scope of library holdings, and economic or demographic characteristics of the population served.

Source: ICMA (1998), p. 4-74.

• Calculate the statistical standard deviation of the values for each indicator and choose a certain number of standard deviations to represent the boundaries between the grades.

The last two approaches (use of percentiles and standard deviations) have the advantage in that they appear scientific and can be supported by the actual data used to calculate them. However, these approaches have a problem similar to the problem with rankings—they are based on *past* actual values and the *relative* positions of the agencies. This is especially true with percentiles, since there is always a top and a bottom percentile regardless of how similar the agencies' values are, or whether the performance levels are all good—or all bad. As a result, even if all the agencies are performing well, some will receive poor ratings.

The use of "expert" judgment to establish the boundary values probably is the more preferred approach. (The experts might even include customers.) However, this procedure requires the most time and effort—and it may be difficult to gain consensus among the experts. For each indicator, the experts should select the numerical boundaries between grades based on their judgment of what is good or bad performance, not based merely on the historical performance of the agencies.

One problem with all of these rating approaches is that for indicator values near the boundaries, small changes in a particular value can move a jurisdiction from one grade to the next. If this appears to be an important problem, it can be alleviated somewhat by using additional "in-between" grades, such as grades A– and B+.

5. *Examine changes from previous years (e.g., time trends).* An important comparison, often neglected in interagency comparisons, examines current performance levels in the light of previous levels. The percentage change from the previous year, or some other base year, can be calculated for each jurisdiction on each indicator. An accurate comparison, however, means that data from multiple years must be obtained using consistent data definitions and collection procedures.

For interjurisdictional comparisons, percentage changes can be calculated and used for a second set of rankings and ratings. This option recognizes not only the importance of absolute values but also the value of improved performance. Agencies, thus, have two opportunities to look good—on the basis of their current performance levels and on the extent of their improvement. Such ranking can motivate agencies that have performed poorly, or believe they might in the future, to participate in comparison efforts.

For some comparisons, it may be worthwhile to look at longer-term time trends. This requires that a consistent set of data from several years is available. The percentage change from a base year to the current year can then be used. See, for example, exhibit 6-1 from the 1998 *Kids Count Data Book*. This report presented both 1985 and 1995 data and the percentage-change values for each of its 10 indicators.

6. *Break out and compare key indicators by major demographic groupings.* Most performance measurement efforts tend to focus only on the aggregate data for each indicator (that is, the agencywide value). Often, however, public officials and the general public find data broken out by major population groups (e.g., age, gender, race/ethnicity, and income) to be more enlightening and useful. Some breakouts, however, will not be useful for intergovernmental comparisons. For example, breakouts by neighborhoods will likely be very suitable for comparisons *within* a city or county, but such comparisons will not likely be relevant among jurisdictions. By contrast, other breakouts can legitimately be compared across agencies and will likely be very informative. For example, comparisons of low-birth-weight babies by the mother's age, income, and ethnic/racial group might be very helpful in identifying which agencies are, or are not, successfully achieving high levels of performance for particular demographic groups. In another example, library circulation and transit-use rates might be broken out and compared by age, gender, and ethnic/racial groups.

Such information can be used to identify those agencies that have performed well in serving specific groups and, subsequently, to identify best practices (as discussed in option 3 in the next section).

7. *Combine scores on individual indicators to provide an overall index of each jurisdiction's performance.* Summary indicators can be used to combine the data from each of a number of separate indicators for a service, or even to combine indicators for all services in a jurisdiction.[1] The resulting index is then compared with the indices calculated for other jurisdictions. These indices can then be presented in the form of ratings or rankings, and perhaps also show any changes from previous years. Average and median indices can also be calculated.

A major issue with such indices is how to "weight" each indicator when calculating the combined index. Most such indices are calculated in the simplest possible way—the index is merely an average of all the rankings or ratings (or the sum of the rankings). *This implicitly assumes that each indicator is of equal value.* Others, such as *U.S. News's* rankings of colleges and universities, assign specific weights to each indicator.

Simplifying the presentation by using indices is tempting. However, this procedure can distort reality if the weights for the indicators do not adequately reflect the relative importance of each component of the index. Such indices, however, are likely to be of particular value for service outcomes that are highly technical, such as air and water quality. In both cases, the indices have many technical components. Users of the information may not be able to interpret the individual components and would otherwise have to rely on the expertise of environmental experts. Combining the components into aggregate air and water quality indices makes it much easier for public officials and the community as a whole to use the information.

If indices are used, the resulting report should provide readers with the following additional information:

- The values for each indicator, so that users themselves can determine the weights that should be given to each of the indicators; and
- The specific weights used in calculating the indices (such as "Each indicator was given equal weight when combining the individual indicators").

Some CPM efforts allow users to modify the weights given to each indicator in order to produce custom rankings. Both *Money* magazine's "Best Places to Live" and *U.S. News's* "America's Best Colleges" efforts provide this capability on their Internet sites.

Further Comments on the Options

- In reports of the findings of any type of analysis, the actual values for every indicator in each jurisdiction should also be presented, if only in appendices. This applies whether the report provides rankings, ratings, or indices. Our preference is to include the data on each indicator in the main body of the report, rather than as appendices, except when the individual indicators are highly technical.

- The seven options listed above are not mutually exclusive. Some, or all, could be combined and used in a report.

- We are somewhat apprehensive about rankings—for the reasons given above—and prefer ratings. However, if the basic data on each indicator for each jurisdiction are also presented, the dangers in ranking can be alleviated.

- Exhibits 6-1 and 6-2 are examples of presentations using a number of the data analysis options. Exhibit 6-1 is a typical example from the *Kids Count Data Book*, showing values on 10 indicators for two particular years (1985 and 1995) and providing rankings for one state relative to all of the other states. In addition to average values (national trend data) for all the states, a percentage change from 1985 to 1995 is also provided for each state and for the average across all states. The report also presents a national composite rank, determined by summing each state's rank on each of the 10 measures and then ranking each state on this composite score.

    Exhibit 6-2, from the International City/County Management Association's *Comparative Performance Measurement: FY 1996 Data Report*, is an example of the data on one of many indicators included in that report. For each indicator, information is provided on the jurisdiction's most recent value, the overall mean and median, the percentage change from the previous year, and the distance each jurisdiction is from the mean. Rankings are not specifically assigned, but the jurisdictions are presented in rank order.

    Neither of the efforts illustrated in exhibits 6-1 and 6-2 use ratings. Exhibit 6-3, however, is an example of rating use from the North Carolina Division of Women's and Children's Health (DWCH) effort to rank counties by their performance on specific indicators (Goldstein 1998; Wolfe 1998). Data on indicator values (in this case, various rates, such as the adolescent pregnancy rate) are presented in one column, while the next column presents county rankings for a particular comparison group (as discussed in chapter 2). A unique feature of this effort is its calculation of each county's improvement in a given indicator over time, which is computed in terms of the current three-year period over the previous three-year period and reported as a percentage increase or decrease. Counties are then ranked according to their improvement in each indicator and assigned an overall cumulative ranking. (DWCH has recently decided, however, not to include the performance of other county offices in its report to a county. Instead, it provides the overall state average and the average for the county's own comparison group.)

- One problem with comparisons using multiple indicators is that often the latest available data on the indicators will come from different years. Delays in tabulating and reporting data for some indicators inevitably occur. Thus, comparison reports need to identify the year to which the data apply for each indicator. Furthermore, the latest data available from different agencies on an indicator are sometimes for different years or time periods. This presents another problem, and usually the solution is to exclude the data from agencies that are not for the year or time period sought.

EXHIBIT 6-3

Example of Data Analysis Using Rankings

Women's Preventive Health Program Rankings for Fiscal Year 1996–97

County	POO #1 (Adolescent Pregnancy Rate)				POO #2 (Percent Repeat Teen Pregnancies)				POO #3 (Percent Women with Short Birth Interval)				POO #4 (Out-of-Wedlock Live Births)		Cumulative Points	Cumulative Rank
	Rate	Rank	Improvement	Rank	Rate	Rank	Improvement	Rank	Rate	Rank	Improvement	Rank	Rate	Rank	CUMRNK	OPRANK
Beaufort	29.5	15	0.51	9	15.7	12	3.97	21	11.2	6	0.87	22	42.67	14	99	17
Bertie	31.4	18	0.95	11	12.9	6	-1.24	5	15.1	22	1.44	23	61.09	24	109	21
Brunswick	27.8	13	0.98	12	16.8	18	-0.52	10	13.2	17	0.07	16	34.84	7	93	16
Carteret	20.1	4	2.22	17	13.6	7	1.95	18	10.7	5	0.01	15	30.1	4	70	4
Craven	24.9	9	-0.28	8	12.4	4	-3.64	3	12.1	10	-0.71	10	28.83	3	47	2
Currituck	18.6	3	2.24	18	17.1	19	3.74	20	13.5	20	-0.89	8	27.96	2	90	11
Dare	13.7	1	4.04	21	17.1	20	10.76	24	10.6	4	0.69	21	24.11	1	92	13
Duplin	33.5	20	2.77	19	14.2	8	-0.69	9	13.4	19	-0.34	13	41.43	13	101	18
Edgecombe	41.1	24	-0.3	7	21.3	23	1.13	16	15.6	23	-0.21	14	60.42	23	130	24
Greene	30.5	17	-2.32	2	17.4	22	3.52	19	12.1	11	0.08	17	45.96	17	105	20
Halifax	36.7	22	3.01	20	16.4	17	-0.91	7	13.2	18	-1.06	6	55.51	22	112	22
Hyde	15.8	2	5.25	22	12.5	5	4.17	23	8.57	1	0.68	20	47.37	18	91	12
Jones	28.4	14	-4.16	1	16.3	16	0.42	13	12.7	15	1.65	24	36.27	9	92	13
Lenoir	40.4	23	1.32	13	23.7	24	0.88	15	14	21	-1.07	5	45.45	16	117	23
Nash	30.1	16	-0.33	6	16.1	13	-3.3	4	12.7	14	-0.91	7	38.39	10	70	4
New Hanover	26.7	12	2.01	14	16.3	15	-1.07	6	12.9	16	-0.4	12	32.03	5	80	8
Northampton	35.3	21	5.62	24	12.1	3	-0.81	8	15.7	24	-1.8	2	53.63	20	102	19
Pamlico	21.2	5	-2.25	3	10	2	-6.22	1	10.2	2	0.28	19	40	11	43	1
Pender	24.8	8	5.31	23	4.21	1	-4.34	2	10.3	3	-1.09	4	34.6	6	47	2
Pitt	31.4	19	2.2	16	14.9	11	-0.2	11	12	9	-1.24	3	40.15	12	81	9
Wayne	26.4	11	2.18	15	17.2	21	0.81	14	12.5	12	-0.61	11	34.99	8	92	13
Hertford-Gates	25	10	-0.91	5	16.2	14	4.07	22	12.6	13	-1.83	1	54.5	21	86	10
MTW	21.5	6	-1.59	4	14.4	9	-0.13	12	11.3	7	0.26	18	52.12	19	75	6
P-P-C-C	22	7	0.82	10	14.8	10	1.17	17	11.5	8	-0.74	9	43.5	15	76	7

(Side label for rows: EAST)

Source: State of North Carolina (1998). Reprinted by permission of the Women's and Children's Health Section, Division of Public Health, North Carolina Department of Health and Human Services.
Note: POO = Process/Outcome Objective.

- Population estimates present a particularly difficult data problem. As indicated in previous chapters, many indicators need to be related to population size in order to make values comparable across agencies. This applies to such indicators as costs per capita, crime, fire, infant mortality, low-weight birth rates, and so on. Because the major census is only taken every 10 years, precise data are not available between decades. The Census Bureau makes regular estimates of state populations and periodic estimates for local governments. State and local governments also participate by providing periodic estimates for certain demographic characteristics. The net result is that methods of estimating population data among jurisdictions are likely to vary, and no perfect solution exists to this problem. This is one of those situations that analysts and information users simply have to live with. Resulting reports, however, need to identify any such problems with the data.
- For presentations of comparison data grouped by performance indicator, the question arises as to whether an indicator should be included in a report if the number of agencies compared is very small. For example, ICMA Local Government CPM Consortium reports include an indicator only if at least 10 jurisdictions provide data on that indicator. The number included is somewhat arbitrary. It can be argued that comparisons are useful even if only two agencies or jurisdictions are compared. However, for reports that are intended for a national readership in particular, some minimum number should be specified, if only to keep down the size of the report. Furthermore, useful statistical information will be considerably limited with very small samples of agencies.

Why Did the Agency Perform That Way?

One of CPM's major purposes is to stimulate agencies to make improvements. Providing information on why some agencies are achieving better results than others can help accomplish this. This section discusses ways to find out why some agencies are performing better (or worse) than others. CPM data only tell agencies *where* they stand relative to others—not *why*. However, important clues as to the "whys" can be gleaned from the comparison process. Following are options for developing information on the reasons various agencies perform differently:

1. *Examine the relationships of key* external *factors to the performance values*. The reasons why some agencies have better outcomes than others are usually quite complex. Nevertheless, analysts should attempt to provide some insights. For example, external factors—those that are not influenced by the agencies—may cause outcome differences. A basic approach to identifying these significant external factors involves using statistical regression analysis to determine the extent of the relationship between individual external factors and the indicator values. Such procedures require some knowledge of statistics; however, procedures are well-known and can usually be readily applied. When a small number of agencies are being compared, normally only one external factor at

EXHIBIT 6-4

Example of an Examination of the Relationship of External Factors to Outcome Data

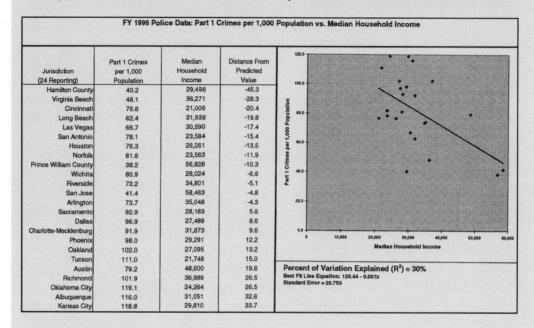

FY 1996 Police Data: Part 1 Crimes per 1,000 Population vs. Median Household Income

Jurisdiction (24 Reporting)	Part 1 Crimes per 1,000 Population	Median Household Income	Distance From Predicted Value
Hamilton County	40.2	29,498	-45.3
Virginia Beach	48.1	36,271	-28.3
Cincinnati	76.6	21,006	-20.4
Long Beach	62.4	31,938	-19.8
Las Vegas	66.7	30,590	-17.4
San Antonio	78.1	23,584	-15.4
Houston	76.3	26,261	-13.5
Norfolk	81.6	23,563	-11.9
Prince William County	38.2	56,828	-10.3
Wichita	80.9	28,024	-6.6
Riverside	73.2	34,801	-5.1
San Jose	41.4	58,463	-4.8
Arlington	73.7	35,048	-4.3
Sacramento	92.9	28,183	5.6
Dallas	96.9	27,489	8.6
Charlotte-Mecklenburg	91.9	31,873	9.6
Phoenix	98.0	29,291	12.2
Oakland	102.0	27,095	13.2
Tucson	111.0	21,748	15.0
Austin	79.2	48,600	19.6
Richmond	101.9	36,989	26.5
Oklahoma City	119.1	24,264	26.5
Albuquerque	116.0	31,051	32.6
Kansas City	118.8	29,810	33.7

Percent of Variation Explained (R^2) = 30%
Best Fit Line Equation: 125.44 - 0.001x
Standard Error = 20.753

Source: ICMA (1998), p. 3-15.

a time should be examined. With large sample sizes, the relationships of more external factors to indicator values can be examined simultaneously.

The external factors most likely to be useful for interagency analysis are various demographic characteristics, such as the percentage of the population defined as low income or below the poverty level. Such factors can affect some performance indicators a great deal and are, for the most part, outside the control of individual agencies. Exhibit 6-4 illustrates the results of one such analysis (from the ICMA *FY 1996 Data Report*) that relates Part 1 crimes per 1,000 population to median household income.

Information from statistical analysis has two important uses. First, it helps identify causal factors. Such analysis does not necessarily determine cause; it primarily indicates correlation. However, sound judgment can be used to identify external factors that other evidence indicates are likely to affect the value of particular indicators and, thus, should be statistically examined.

A second and very important use of information from statistical analysis involves making adjustments to agency rankings and ratings, allowing for fairer comparisons. This is done by ranking and rating the agencies based not on the actual values, but on the values expected after adjusting for explanatory factors—that is, the distance that each jurisdiction is from the line of best fit becomes the criterion for ratings and rankings (exhibit 6-4). Those agencies performing much better than the values expected are ranked, and rated, highest. The rankings shown in exhibit 6-4 are different from rankings based on actual values (without adjustments for median household income). For example, Cincinnati moved from 11th out of 26 to

3rd out of 24 jurisdictions. (Data on median household income were not available for 2 of the 26 jurisdictions.)

Even the media use regression analysis on occasion. In a 1999 article on Maryland school test scores, the *Washington Post* reported:

> Using a statistical technique called multiple regression analysis, the *Post* estimated how closely actual 1997–98 Maryland School Performance Assessment Program scores correlated with student income and other factors beyond the control of educators. It then used the results of that study to estimate how much higher or lower each school's actual scores were on the MSPAP tests than the schools' "predicted" scores. Schools whose actual scores topped their predicted score by a big margin may well be doing a good job of educating their students—even if the actual raw scores were only average (Argetsinger 1999a).

In this example, the outcome data on regular test scores from different schools (breakout data), along with explanatory characteristics (such as the proxy for student income "percentage of students eligible for free or reduced-price lunches"), were used to provide fairer and more detailed information on school performance. Other states and their individual school districts can, and should, use such analysis. In addition, similar analyses can be conducted by many public and private organizations.

Another example of the use of explanatory characteristics comes from the Third International Mathematics and Science Study (TIMMS). Its reports include tables identifying factors associated with the relatively poor performance of the United States as compared with the other participating countries (see exhibit 6-5). Characteristics examined included such external factors as "average hours watching TV or videos," "average hours working at a paid job on a normal school day," and "hours of homework."

A statistic that is probably most helpful in determining whether an important relationship exists between an external factor and performance values is the "coefficient of determination." It identifies the percentage of variation among the indicator values that is explained by the external factor. For a given CPM effort, analysts need to select a percentage below which they believe the external factor explains enough of the variation to be important. For the ICMA effort (exhibit 6-4), Urban Institute and ICMA staff selected 15 percent as the cutoff point. If the external factor explained at least 15 percent of the variation, the relationship was felt to be significant and was reported. (Note: To our knowledge, no scientific agreement exists as to what the cutoff point should be.) Thus, from the data as shown in exhibit 6-4, it is likely that the external factor (in this example, median household income) in some way accounts for the differences in the value of the performance indicator (in this case, Part 1 crime rates).

2. *Relate indicator values to key internal factors that appear likely to affect indicator values.* This option follows the same procedure as the previous one, which discussed relating indicator values to external factors. Internal factors are those factors over which the agency can reasonably be expected to have considerable

EXHIBIT 6-5

Example of a Presentation of Explanatory Information

RELATIONSHIP BETWEEN U.S. RELATIVE PERFORMANCE AND SCHOOLING AND STUDENT FACTORS:
MATHEMATICS GENERAL KNOWLEDGE

FACTORS	U.S. COMPARED TO INTERNATIONAL AVERAGE OR MOST COMMON PATTERN ON THE FACTOR[1]	FACTOR ASSOCIATED WITH U.S. RELATIVE PERFORMANCE[2]	APPENDIX TABLE WITH SUPPORTING INFORMATION
MATHEMATICS GENERAL KNOWLEDGE			
DIFFERENTIATION IN SCHOOLS/PROGRAMS	LESS	NO	A5.12
DIFFERENTIATION IN LENGTH OF SECONDARY EDUCATION	LESS	NO	A5.12
AVERAGE AGE OF STUDENTS PARTICIPATING IN THE ASSESSMENT	BELOW	YES	A5.13
GRADE OF STUDENTS ASSESSED	SAME	NO	A5.13
CURRENT ENROLLMENT IN SECONDARY EDUCATION	SAME	NO	A5.14
SECONDARY COMPLETION AMONG 25-34 YEAR OLDS	ABOVE	NO	A5.14
CURRICULAR GRADE-LEVEL EQUIVALENT OF THE ASSESSMENT	ABOVE	—	NONE
CENTRALIZATION OF DECISION-MAKING ABOUT CURRICULUM SYLLABI	LESS	NO	A5.15
GNP PER CAPITA	ABOVE	NO	A5.16
PUBLIC EXPENDITURE ON ELEMENTARY/SECONDARY EDUCATION PER CAPITA	ABOVE	NO	A5.16
TAKING MATHEMATICS IN FINAL YEAR OF SECONDARY SCHOOL	BELOW	NO	A5.20
HOURS OF HOMEWORK	BELOW	NO	A5.20
DAILY USE OF CALCULATORS	SAME	NO	A5.20
CALCULATOR USE ON TIMSS	BELOW	YES	A5.20
USE OF COMPUTERS	ABOVE	NO	A5.20
POSITIVE ATTITUDES TOWARD MATHEMATICS	ABOVE	NO	A5.20
THEFT OF PROPERTY AT SCHOOL	ABOVE	NO	A5.20
PERSONAL THREATS AT SCHOOL	ABOVE	NO	A5.20
AVERAGE HOURS WATCHING TV OR VIDEOS	SAME	NO	A5.20
AVERAGE HOURS WORKING AT A PAID JOB ON A NORMAL SCHOOL DAY	ABOVE	NO	A5.20

— Data not available.

1. Based on how the United States compares to the international average for the TIMSS countries for which data were available.

2. Based on whether the factor was associated with the relatively poor performance of the United States compared to the other participating countries.

SOURCES: Mullis et al. (1998). *Mathematics and Science Achievement in the Final Year of Secondary School.* Chestnut Hill, MA: Boston College; and Organisation for Economic Cooperation and Development. (1997). *Education at a Glance: OECD Indicators 1997.* Paris: OECD.

Source: Takahira et al. (1998), p. 69.

influence. This step can help agencies identify service practices and policies that appear to affect results. Such factors include, for example, whether the agency contracts for or self-administers its service; staff-customer ratios; and the extent of the use of specific service delivery procedures or materials, such as particular construction materials for road paving or types of water or sewer pipes.

Adjusting rankings or ratings for internal factors is *not*, however, appropriate for making comparisons more equitable. Even if analysts find a substantial relationship between an internal factor and an indicator value, that information should normally *not* be used to alter agency rankings and ratings. Adjusting for the value of the *external* factors enhances the fairness and, therefore, the validity of the comparisons. Adjustments for *internal* factors influenced by the agencies are not appropriate, since these factors are merely policy and practice choices made by the individual agencies.

In order to use this option, analysts need first to identify which factors seem likely to have an effect on performance and then to obtain data from each participating agency on each of these internal factors. For example, the TIMSS effort examined internal factors—characteristics associated with schools— in its analysis of U.S. relative performance in math and science. The school-related characteristics examined include public expenditure on elementary and secondary education per capita; differences in length of secondary education; and centralization of decisionmaking about curriculum (see exhibit 6-5). Some characteristics examined, such as students' "daily use of calculators" and "use of computers," combine internal and external characteristics, since they may include use of calculators in or out of school.

3. *Seek information from agencies identified as outliers to determine "best practices."* There are a number of ways to select these outliers, including the following:

- Select a *specific number of agencies*, such as the three top-ranked agencies.
- Select only those outliers that are *beyond some number of statistical standard deviations* from the average value.[2]
- *Examine visually how the values are clustered.* For example, see exhibit 6-2, from ICMA's 1996 CPM report. The top four jurisdictions appear to have substantially more annual circulation per capita than the rest. The analysts might ask for "best practice" information from only the top two jurisdictions, or they might cast a wider net and seek information from the top four jurisdictions. The decision as to the number of jurisdictions to query is a matter of judgment.

After outliers have been identified, each jurisdiction should be asked to verify the accuracy of its data and to identify practices and policies staff believe have contributed to the high level of performance. (Unfortunately, this step is seldom performed.) Findings from the agencies might be reported individually, or the analysts might look for, and report on, patterns in the responses. The Local Government Performance Measurement Consortium experimented with this approach in its reports for fiscal years 1995 and 1996. ICMA identified those city and county agencies that appeared to have "better" levels of per-

EXHIBIT 6-6

Sample Memo Requesting Successful Practices Information

TO: [Appropriate Agency]

FROM: [Sponsor]

RE: Good Performance Outcomes for [agency name] and Request for Successful Practices Information

A review of [type of service—e.g., police, fire, etc.] services data indicates that [jurisdiction name] has had particularly good outcomes on the following performance indicators(s):

- [indicator name(s) and value(s)—e.g., average response time to emergency calls—xx minutes]

The identification of successful practices can be a major benefit from interagency comparison data.

Would you please review the indicator(s) above and answer the following questions:

1. Are the data correct?
2. Are there any unique circumstances in your agency or jurisdiction, or factors beyond your agency's control (such as climate or population characteristics), that you believe explain this high level of performance?

OR

3. Does your agency have in place one or more specific practices or innovations (such as procedures, policies, equipment, etc.) that you believe likely explains the high level of performance? If so, please provide a description of that practice, plus the name and phone number of the person to whom any follow-up questions should be addressed.

Please provide this information by fax or e-mail as soon as possible, but no later than [date representing 10 business days from expected receipt of memo]. Successful practices will be highlighted in our [year] published report.

Many thanks.

---

formance and asked them to identify any policies or practices they felt had contributed to that high level of performance.

Exhibit 6-6 is a version of a memo used to request such information. The memo first asks the jurisdiction to verify that the data used to determine the indicator values for the jurisdiction were correct and, if correct, to identify any special circumstances in the jurisdiction that might have caused the performance to be as high as it was. If neither of these apply, the jurisdiction is then asked to identify practices or policies it believes contributed to the high level of performance.

This same process can be used in any interagency comparison. The weakness of this procedure is that it depends heavily on the agencies' ability to correctly identify the policies and practices related to their high level of performance. As will be discussed later, a more in-depth examination of successful practices and policies is preferable to identify reasons for the high performance.

When seeking such "best practices" information, it is better to *select outliers that have demonstrated high levels of performance for more than one year*. This is possible for interjurisdictional comparisons that are repeated on a regular basis. Analysts might use two or three years' worth of data to identify agencies for follow-up, then look for patterns in the responses and report them.

4. *Examine the reasons for low performance levels.* This might be done using the same procedure described to identify high performers. Requesting reasons for low performance, however, is likely to be sensitive. We know of no instances where this has been done as part of interagency comparison studies. Nonetheless, conceptually it seems to be a useful step, because agencies can learn from the experiences of low performers as well as high performers.

5. *Undertake special in-depth studies to identify reasons for high or low performance levels.* As indicated previously, data analyses can provide some limited information, or clues, as to the reasons for high or low performance. However, to really get at the reasons in a substantial, comprehensive manner, more in-depth examination is needed.

Such studies might be done by individual agencies or by a third-party organization. Individual agencies are likely to take a limited look, focusing on only a small number of other agencies—perhaps by writing, phoning, or otherwise communicating with these other agencies in an attempt to identify their practices and policies.

A third-party organization, such as a professional association, a higher-level government agency, or a university, might have resources to undertake or sponsor a more systematic study, examining many agencies in order to detect reasons for high (or low) performance. Such studies would likely examine many external and internal factors.

Either way, such studies preferably would be undertaken by a combination of agency personnel and experts in the subject area. An example of "best practice reviews," while not based on past performance data, is the work of Minnesota's Office of the Legislative Auditor. These reviews were performed on selected local government services, using a local government advisory committee (State of Minnesota 1998).

Finally, some agencies might reexamine their own efforts in order to find ways to improve what they are doing rather than seek information from agencies with higher performance levels.

The options listed above represent at least a first cut at steps that can be taken to analyze comparative data. As the field of CPM expands, as it undoubtedly will, given the exploding interest in performance measurement at all levels of governments and in the private nonprofit sector, analysts can be expected to develop many other options.

Notes

1. For a detailed discussion of index development and use, see Gormley and Weimer (1999).
2. One standard deviation in a normally distributed set of agencies would be expected to contain approximately 16 percent of the agencies—in the favorable direction. Two standard deviations would be expected to contain approximately 2.4 percent of the agencies.

Chapter 7

Presentation is half the battle in encouraging readers to use the information.

Reporting CPM Information

This chapter discusses what usually is the final step in an intergovernmental CPM effort—reporting the information. This step involves identifying report customers, determining the content and format for the report, and, finally, deciding what to report if the news is "bad."

Customers for the Comparison Report

The persons likely to have the greatest interest in the report are the managers of the agencies being compared. They have the most at stake. Other likely interested parties include:

- Other personnel in the agencies being compared;
- Other officials who oversee the agencies being compared, including elected or appointed officials;
- Media in each location that includes an agency being compared;
- Managers and officials of agencies not included in the comparisons who believe they are doing work similar to that being done by the comparison agencies and who want to compare their own agency's performance with the data in the report; and
- Public interest groups and the general public, depending on the topics covered by the report.

Most interagency comparison reports will be publicly available; therefore, readability and accessibility are major considerations. On occasion, a primarily internal effort, such as an agency's own collection of data from a few other agencies, may not be published or otherwise available.

It is important to make customers aware that the report is available and accessible. Agencies that contributed information to the effort and are included in the comparisons will, of course, be aware of the report. If not, they are likely to hear about the report from another agency or the media. Web posting enhances accessibility even further, at least for those persons with Internet access. Report sponsors should arrange for copies to be placed in the public libraries serving the jurisdictions included in the report. Of course, agencies that fare poorly in the comparisons may prefer as little accessibility as possible (see the discussion of what to do if the news is bad later in the chapter).

Content of the Report

CPM reports need to provide full information on what the data mean and their limitations. Exhibit 7-1 summarizes the content of an ideal report. Specific directions relating to the material included in these reports are listed below.

1. *Clearly and thoroughly define each indicator*. A brief definition should be provided when the data are presented. A more complete definition, if necessary, can be included in an appendix.

EXHIBIT 7-1

Suggested Contents of the Report

A comparative performance report should include the following elements:

1. Introductory section on the background, purposes, and uses of the data. This section should also contain a prominent discussion of the limitations of the data, what the data do not tell, and any concerns relating to the data's quality.
2. A section describing the information provided, the procedures used to obtain the data, and any special analytic methods used. If the report is one in a series being presented at regular intervals, any differences from previous reports should be identified, such as different indicators, additions or subtractions to the categories of data provided, and improvements in any of the comparison procedures.
3. A table depicting the key characteristics of each agency being compared, such as total expenditures and the number of employees, in order to help readers better interpret the performance data. Sometimes organizational characteristics might be important; for example, when comparing state government social service agencies, the reader should know whether a particular agency is state or locally administered. Such information can provide a better context for data interpretation.
4. A list of indicators for which data are presented. This will help readers see at one glance what performance indicators are included in the report.
5. A section reporting the comparative data—normally the major part of the report (see chapter 6).
6. A section describing findings as to the relationships between explanatory factors and the performance indicator values.
7. Successful practices information obtained from the agencies (see chapter 6).
8. A glossary of terms. The glossary should provide definitions and calculation procedures for indicators used in the report.

---

2. *Include the source and date of the data for each indicator, perhaps in brief footnotes on the tables or charts.* More extensive information can be provided in an appendix. (The federal government frequently includes back-up appendixes that describe the source and nature of data in major data reports, such as those reports produced by the U.S. Bureau of Census, U.S. Department of Health and Human Services, and U.S. Department of Education. For examples, see the annual *Condition of Education* report [Department of Education] and *America's Children: Key National Indicators of Well-Being,* published by the Federal InterAgency Forum on Child and Family Statistics. Not all these reports provide data comparing jurisdictions, such as individual states. Nevertheless, these reports set a high standard for describing [in appendixes] the individual indicators and how the data were obtained.)

3. *If only a subset of the relevant agencies are covered, furnish the rationale for agency selection—along with implications for interpreting the data.* For example, the agencies selected might be only those of a certain size or only those for which data are available, or CPM sponsors might not have sufficient resources to cover all the agencies. In the latter case, the report should clearly indicate how the sample was chosen, such as by random sampling or some other selection procedure.

4. *Do not present rankings and ratings (such as grades) without also providing the basic data from which these rankings and ratings were derived.* Preferably, the basic data should be included in the body of the report so that readers can better interpret differences among rankings and ratings. These data normally should be considered a major part of the findings, while the rankings and ratings aid the reader in assessing where individual agencies stand—both in absolute terms (ratings) and relative to each other (rankings and ratings.) If ratings are used (such as "report card" grades of A, B, and C, etc.), the basis for these rating categories should also be identified.

5. *Similarly, when indices are used to combine a number of indicators, supply the data on each indicator included in the index and explain how the values were combined to generate the index.* For example, if the index is a simple arithmetic average of the ranks of the individual indicators (as is commonly done), this should be so stated, pointing out that this procedure assumes that each indicator is of equal importance.

6. *Include caveats about the data.* Inevitably, comparison data will have many limitations and technical problems. Comparisons that require the agencies themselves to collect and provide data mean that differences in data collection procedures inevitably will occur. (This was certainly true with the data from the jurisdictions that participated in the Local Government CPM Consortium, even though considerable data cleaning efforts, such as those described in chapter 5, took place). Even for those efforts for which data have been collected by a single agency (such as population data obtained by the U.S. Bureau of the Census), problems in data collection inevitably exist (such as missed families).

   For CPM reports in which the data are grouped by indicators, such caveats might be included on the pages containing the data. The information on the lower part of exhibit 6-2 illustrates one way to identify such concerns.

Readers should also be advised that the indicators included are inevitably highly selective. The data presented in any one report cannot show all of the performance information likely to be relevant to the services on which the agencies are being compared. Readers should also be cautioned that performance information tells only what the outcomes were, not *why* those outcomes resulted.

In addition, readers should be reminded to *consider the magnitude of differences* among agencies, especially when rankings are used. As discussed in the previous chapter, small differences can exist among the agencies being examined. When drawing conclusions from the data, readers should decide whether small differences in indicator values are important.

7. *Present explanatory information wherever possible.* As noted previously, a major gap in most reporting efforts is that interagency comparison efforts seldom explain why the data are the way they are. Chapter 6 suggested some options that those undertaking these comparisons might try to at least partially fill this void. Most efforts comparing data across agencies are highly limited in their resources and tend to stop short of explanatory information.

   Such information for each indicator might include identification of each explanatory factor examined (e.g., population per square mile), the percentage of variation explained by that factor (the R^2 value), the number of jurisdictions reporting, the direction of the relationship (positive or negative), and whether that factor is external or internal to the agency. (See the ICMA *FY 1996 Data Report* for examples of such presentations.) This information can help readers identify the extent to which various factors believed to have explanatory power were actually found to be explanatory, given the available data.

   The simplest approach, illustrated in exhibit 6-2, is to identify some possible causes, even if only in a general way. Even more important, as described in chapter 6, is to secure explanatory information from high performers as to the policies and practices they believe contributed to their high performance levels.

   Such explanatory information can make comparison reports much more interesting and useful and greatly enhance the value of CPM efforts. The more agencies share their experiences with various service delivery approaches, the more they can learn from each other.

8. *Present selected statistical data, including the results of statistical analyses that relate explanatory factors to individual indicators.* While statistical data may be overly technical for some users, such data can considerably enhance perspectives on the findings for others. Statistical regression analysis charts might be included for each explanatory factor that appears significantly related to an indicator (as discussed in chapter 6 and illustrated in exhibit 6-3) and might provide the following information:

   - A table listing the agencies in rank order, *with the ranks based on the distance of each agency's values from the statistically derived "expected values."* For each jurisdiction, the table should show the specific amount by which actual value differs from expected value, indicating the values for both the performance indicator and the explanatory factor.
   - The number of agencies that provided data on both the performance indicator and the explanatory factor.

- The percentage of the variation among agencies explained by the explanatory factor (the "R square" value, also called the "coefficient of determination") and the "standard error" of the statistical relationship. (The latter helps identify the way the values for the indicator are distributed.)
- A "scatter" diagram that plots the values for each agency as they relate to the explanatory factor (see exhibit 6-3). This diagram provides a picture of the way the actual values are distributed around the predicted values and should include the statistically derived "regression line" that best fits the values plotted for the agencies. This line represents the expected value of the performance indicator for each agency, given the value of the explanatory factor. The vertical distance from the agency's actual value to the line indicates how far the actual value is above or below the expected value. The numerical value of that distance is listed in the table accompanying the scatter diagram, as noted above.
- Explanatory text to help the reader understand the data presented. This text might be included on the bottom of the page containing the statistical chart and should summarize the nature of the relationship depicted in the chart, for example, "This chart indicates that the performance indicator tended to be lower in agencies that had a higher value of the explanatory factor." The text should also identify other factors likely to have caused variations in that indicator, including possible differences in how agencies defined or reported the indicator or explanatory factor.

Format of the Report

Presentation is half the battle in encouraging readers to use the information. With today's information technology, even small agencies can prepare attractive, user-friendly reports. Nevertheless, many organizations, especially governments and their agencies, tend to produce crowded and difficult-to-read reports.[1]

The degree of polishing the format needs depends to a great extent on the audience. Reports intended strictly for internal use do not need to be as refined as those intended for elected officials and the general public. However, all reports should meet basic standards of user-friendliness and understandability. Exhibits 6-1 and 6-2 (see chapter 6) are examples of formats that should be considered (in addition to text material). Successful formats should include a variety of graphic aids, including:

- tables
- bar charts
- line charts
- maps

Each is discussed briefly below.

Tables

Tables can provide more data in a limited space than other approaches. Their disadvantage is that, except for data-oriented readers, tables are often not user friendly. Yet despite this, they are frequently the best way to present the basic data users need to understand the material. Table titles, along with row and column headings, need to be clearly specified. Tables can be included as appendixes if they make the main body of the report overly detailed.

Bar Charts

Bar charts (see exhibits 6-1 and 6-2) are a common way to show comparative data. They provide readers with a quick visual sense of the range of data and relative standing of each agency being compared. Including numerical values enables readers to readily identify each agency's level of performance without having to estimate those values by interpolation from axis numbers. The disadvantage of bar charts, as compared with tables, is that they take up considerably more space.

Before a report is finalized, bar charts should be visually scanned in order to identify incorrect data (due to interpretation or definition differences, or to clerical error). Values for one jurisdiction that appear much better or much worse than all the other jurisdictions need to be checked before the data are officially reported. (See the discussion of data quality control in chapter 5.)

Bar charts visually depict the comparative values for each performance indicator. The bars for each agency should be arrayed with the better values at the top. Note, however, that for some performance indicators, the better values are the highest values; for others, they are the lowest. For some indicators, therefore, higher values will appear at the bottom of the chart (such as those for indicators of crime rates and response times).

Bar charts should include full identification of the indicator and the year for which data are presented. We recommend that such charts include the following information:

- The distance each agency is from the average (mean) value of all the reporting jurisdictions.
- Basic statistics—the mean (average) of all reported values; the median value of all reported values; and the standard deviation (which provides information about how the values are distributed).
- The percentage change from the previous year, with a plus (+) or minus (−) sign to indicate that the value has increased or decreased. The plus or minus sign relates to an increase or decrease in the value of the indicator, not to whether performance has improved or declined. This should be made clear to readers. (As noted above, in some cases, improved performance is associated with a decrease in the value of the indicator.) When comparable data for more than two years are available, the chart should show changes from more than one past year. This can be done by including two columns, one showing the change (or value) from the previous year and the second showing the change (or value) from two years ago, or from a previous base year.
- Explanatory text (a "caption") to help the reader understand the data presented. The text should include clarification of terms (e.g., "percentage of

crimes cleared") or an explanation of how the indicator was calculated, if not obvious. Likely explanations for differences among agencies should also be included in the caption, focusing on major explanatory factors—particularly those that are not controlled by the agency (external factors). Preferably the explanatory text should be placed at the bottom of the page containing the bar chart—or on the facing page if space limitations preclude the former.

In exhibit 6-1, bar charts display the extent of the percentage changes from 1985 to 1995 for each of the 10 indicators, including *national* changes.

Line Charts

Exhibit 7-2 illustrates line charts, which can be an excellent way to summarize data on a large number of performance indicators in a small amount of space. The charts shown here *summarize* the fiscal year 1996 data for one jurisdiction participating in the ICMA Local Government CPM Consortium. The report itself includes data on the individual performance indicators, showing each jurisdiction's performance values (see exhibit 6-2). Line charts were prepared to summarize each jurisdiction's own data across all the indicators. Thus, exhibit 7-2 presents data on a large number of indicators for one jurisdiction. These charts show the range of values for all the participating jurisdictions, the average of all jurisdictions, and the value for the particular jurisdiction.

Line charts permit readers interested in a particular agency to quickly examine the findings for large numbers of indicators and easily determine those indicators for which the agency demonstrated high or low levels of performance. The agency itself can then select indicators that warrant recognition or further attention.

Maps

Because CPM data generally involve data from jurisdictions in different geographic areas, it is particularly appropriate and useful to present these data on maps. As mapping software has become more common and easy to use, spatial presentation of data has become more widespread. Maps allow higher-level governments (state or federal) to readily see geographic or regional concentrations of good or poor outcomes and take action to address problems. Spatial presentation also may increase citizen or media understanding of and interest in comparative data. The old adage "A picture is worth 1,000 words" applies to maps as well.

Exhibit 7-3, from the Annie E. Casey Foundation's 1998 *Kids Count Data Book*, illustrates the presentation of comparative data on a map of the United States. Maps like this one make it easy to identify clusters or concentrations of states with either high or low performance in terms of a particular indicator (in this case, percentage of low-birth-weight babies). Maps generally use different

(text continues on page 86)

EXHIBIT 7-2

Example of a Line Chart Summarizing One Jurisdiction's Performance on Multiple Indicators

FY 1996 Neighborhood Services Indicators: Comparative Performance Measurement
Arlington, Texas

ROAD MAINTENANCE

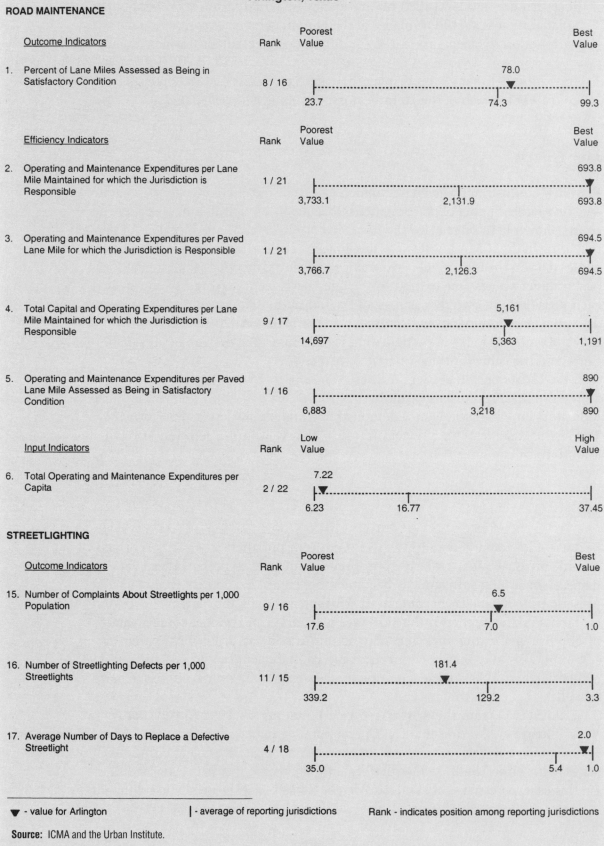

			Poorest Value		Best Value
Outcome Indicators		Rank			
1.	Percent of Lane Miles Assessed as Being in Satisfactory Condition	8 / 16	23.7	78.0 / 74.3	99.3
Efficiency Indicators		Rank	Poorest Value		Best Value
2.	Operating and Maintenance Expenditures per Lane Mile Maintained for which the Jurisdiction is Responsible	1 / 21	3,733.1	2,131.9	693.8 / 693.8
3.	Operating and Maintenance Expenditures per Paved Lane Mile for which the Jurisdiction is Responsible	1 / 21	3,766.7	2,126.3	694.5 / 694.5
4.	Total Capital and Operating Expenditures per Lane Mile Maintained for which the Jurisdiction is Responsible	9 / 17	14,697	5,161 / 5,363	1,191
5.	Operating and Maintenance Expenditures per Paved Lane Mile Assessed as Being in Satisfactory Condition	1 / 16	6,883	3,218	890 / 890
Input Indicators		Rank	Low Value		High Value
6.	Total Operating and Maintenance Expenditures per Capita	2 / 22	7.22 / 6.23	16.77	37.45

STREETLIGHTING

			Poorest Value		Best Value
Outcome Indicators		Rank			
15.	Number of Complaints About Streetlights per 1,000 Population	9 / 16	17.6	6.5 / 7.0	1.0
16.	Number of Streetlighting Defects per 1,000 Streetlights	11 / 15	339.2	181.4 / 129.2	3.3
17.	Average Number of Days to Replace a Defective Streetlight	4 / 18	35.0	5.4	2.0 / 1.0

▼ - value for Arlington | - average of reporting jurisdictions   Rank - indicates position among reporting jurisdictions

Source: ICMA and the Urban Institute.

EXHIBIT 7-3

Example of Using Maps to Display Performance Information

Percent low birth-weight babies*
1995

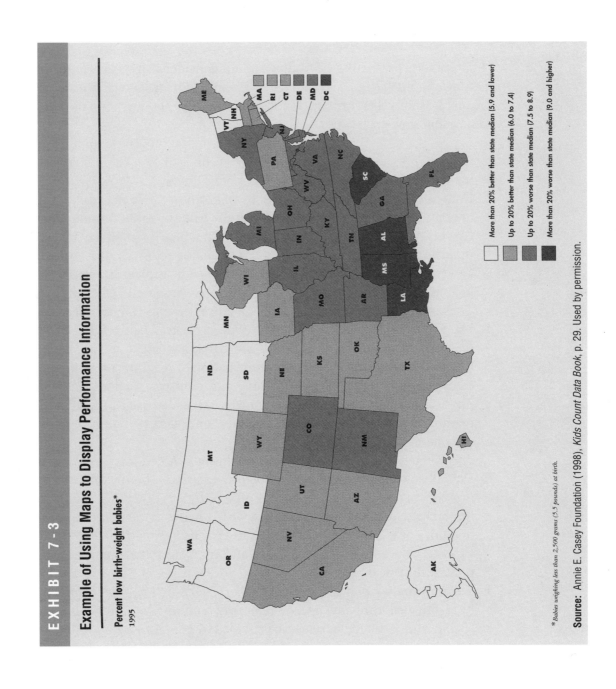

More than 20% better than state median (5.9 and lower)

Up to 20% better than state median (6.0 to 7.4)

Up to 20% worse than state median (7.5 to 8.9)

More than 20% worse than state median (9.0 and higher)

Babies weighing less than 2,500 grams (5.5 pounds) at birth.

Source: Annie E. Casey Foundation (1998), *Kids Count Data Book*, p. 29. Used by permission.

colors or shading to depict specific ranges for the data reported. Similarly, mapping data can be useful for within-state CPM data by showing variations in indicators across counties and within-state concentrations of good or poor performance.

Other Suggestions on Formats

Organizations presenting CPM data should consider using each of the above formatting options. The ideal report uses a combination of some, if not all, of these approaches. Many other formats (not discussed above) also are possible; following are some additional suggestions:

1. *Graphic presentations*, perhaps using color, can be very effective, but they make reproduction considerably more expensive.
2. *Data can be organized by agency or by indicator, or both*. Exhibit 6-1 illustrates data presented by agency, with indicator values grouped under each agency (in this case, each jurisdiction). Reports can also group agencies under each indicator, as shown in exhibit 6-2. The major reports released by the Local Government CPM Consortium were grouped by indicator, but special reports in line chart format (exhibit 7-2) were also prepared for each jurisdiction. These summarized a jurisdiction's own performance on each indicator.
3. *Many, if not most, public (and private) agencies need more effective communication with their citizens*. This means more than just clear and attractive presentations. It also requires selecting information of real interest to the public. For example, most citizens are probably not concerned about data comparing physical output (e.g., number of miles of street repaired). Comparative information on service outcomes and quality, on the other hand, is likely to be of considerably more interest.
4. *Agencies can all be combined or grouped by important agency characteristics*. For example, agencies might be grouped by their size, by the size of the population they serve, by region of the country, or by any other characteristic deemed important enough to provide users with a better understanding of the information. For example, the FBI's *Uniform Crime Reports* indicate the number of various crimes by individual cities and then combine them for each metropolitan statistical area.
5. *The performance of a particular agency (or jurisdiction, region, or country) can be highlighted using an "agency-centered" reporting format*. Exhibit 7-2 is one such example. Such charts were provided by ICMA to each participating local government as a supplement to the FY 1996 consolidated comparison report. Another example is the work of the Third International Mathematics and Science Study (TIMMS), which presents many of its data in a way that makes it easy to compare the performance of the United States with that of other countries (U.S. Department of Education 1998). For example, exhibit 7-4 groups nations in terms of whether their average scores (in science general knowledge, in this case) are significantly higher than, significantly lower than, or not significantly different from U.S. scores.

EXHIBIT 7-4

Example of an "Agency-Centered" Reporting Format

SCIENCE GENERAL KNOWLEDGE ACHIEVEMENT

NATIONS WITH AVERAGE SCORES SIGNIFICANTLY HIGHER THAN THE U.S.	
NATION	AVERAGE
SWEDEN	559
(NETHERLANDS)	558
(ICELAND)	549
(NORWAY)	544
(CANADA)	532
NEW ZEALAND	529
(AUSTRALIA)	527
SWITZERLAND	523
(AUSTRIA)	520
(SLOVENIA)	517
(DENMARK)	509

INTERNATIONAL AVERAGE = 500

NATIONS WITH AVERAGE SCORES NOT SIGNIFICANTLY DIFFERENT FROM THE U.S.	
NATION	AVERAGE
(GERMANY)	497
(FRANCE)	487
CZECH REPUBLIC	487
(RUSSIAN FEDERATION)	481
(UNITED STATES)	**480**
(ITALY)	475
HUNGARY	471
(LITHUANIA)	461

NATIONS WITH AVERAGE SCORES SIGNIFICANTLY LOWER THAN THE U.S.	
NATION	AVERAGE
(CYPRUS)	448
(SOUTH AFRICA)	349

NOTE: Nations not meeting international sampling and other guidelines are shown in parentheses.

SOURCE: Mullis et al. (1998). *Mathematics and Science Achievement in the Final Year of Secondary School.* Table 2.2. Chestnut Hill, MA: Boston College.

EXAMPLE 4: SCIENCE GENERAL KNOWLEDGE ITEM

Some high-heeled shoes are claimed to damage floors. The base diameter of these very high heels is about 0.5 cm and of ordinary heels about 3 cm. Briefly explain why the very high heels may cause damage to floors.

Correct Answer Examples:

- *"The pressure from the heel is greater because the area is smaller."*

- *"Because of the narrow diameter of very high heels, all the body weight is spread over a smaller area. There is greater pressure exerted on the floor with the higher heels because it is all placed on a small area. The pressure is less on a wider heel because the weight is distributed over a greater area causing less damage."*

U.S. Average: **42 percent**   International Average: **61 percent**

SOURCE: Third International Mathematics and Science Study, 1994-1995.

Source: Takahira et al. (1998), p. 36.

6. *For some comparisons, it may be appropriate not to identify the indicator values for individual agencies.* This may be the preferred option if the agencies were promised confidentiality in return for their data. If confidentiality would not be compromised, the report might *show the individual values for each compared agency without naming the agencies* (i.e., naming them Agency A, Agency B, etc. instead). This would still enable readers to see visually (such as in bar charts) the extent to which agencies differed. Most anonymity will be maintained if the data for *the agencies being compared are only presented in statistical terms,* such as the range of values, the grouped average, the median, and the standard deviation.

What to Report If the News Is Bad

The findings from CPM efforts will inevitably contain some bad news. Most agencies will show up badly on at least some indicators when compared with other agencies, and agency officials will, understandably, be highly concerned about public release of that information. CPM reports will almost always contain public information that at some point needs to be, and should be, released to the community. What should an agency do in situations where the data show what appears to be bad news? The following are some options:

1. *Do nothing—and merely release the comparative data.* And "let the chips fall where they may." This is not necessarily an unreasonable strategy, as long as the agency does not selectively issue the data in such a way that only good news is presented. In the long run, the latter approach is likely to decrease credibility and public trust. The remaining options are usually more appropriate than releasing data without comment.
2. *Provide a summary, highlights, or a report on the comparisons.* Release of CPM data, as with the release of any performance data, should generally be accompanied by some form of public statement or press release. Media and citizen advisers to the Local Government CPM Consortium repeatedly emphasized that these releases should be balanced. That is, releases should not suppress instances where the agency appears to be doing poorly and report only instances of success. Public officials are generally reluctant to present bad news, but ultimately a balanced strategy appears to be the best strategy and most likely to increase credibility and public trust.
3. *Include in the highlights report any planned actions, and any action already under way, aimed at correcting problems identified in the comparative performance report.* This should help increase media and public confidence in the agency's work. The agency should be prepared, however, to describe the results of its corrective actions when subsequent comparison reports are released. Over the long run, it is hoped that high-level public officials will temper the political nature in which performance information is often handled. They should not

"shoot the messenger" when news is bad. Continuing effort is needed in most agencies in order to educate officials, managers, the media, and the public about what CPM data tell and what they do not tell.

Note

1. For suggestions on presentation of data, see Tufte (1992).

Using Comparative Performance Information

Comparative performance measurement provides points of reference that program managers can use to identify areas where their organization is performing well and areas that need improvement.

This chapter discusses some of the many uses for comparative performance information. While these uses apply primarily to the organizations (public or private) covered in a CPM effort, organizations not included can also use the information for many of the same purposes (e.g., to set their own performance targets based in part on the performance levels achieved by other similar agencies). Before using data for any of the purposes discussed below, they should be carefully checked for accuracy.

Applying the Information

1. *Institute corrective actions.* For those performance indicators whose values indicate a pattern of *low performance,* agency administrators should review with responsible personnel the reasons for such performance. Ideally, this process will lead to the development of an action plan for improving performance. Subsequent monitoring of the indicators can assess whether improvements occur or whether additional corrective actions are needed.

   The use of interjurisdictional comparisons in identifying the need for corrective action is particularly appropriate for agencies (especially state and federal agencies) that support or oversee the work of many other agencies. For example, for some programs, such as the (former) Job Training Partnership Act program, the federal government examines CPM data on states' performance in operating a federal program through the states. States with relatively poor CPM performance might therefore be provided with technical assistance or training. Such data also might be used to trigger stronger corrective action, where appropriate. Some states, such as Maryland and New Jersey, are beginning to use school performance data to identify school districts for potential state takeover (see chapter 2) (Argetsinger 1999b). Similarly, North Carolina's Division of Women's and Children's Health uses comparative performance data to identify counties in need of technical assistance or, if poor performance persists, where alternate agencies might be used to provide services.

If the higher-level government shares the CPM data with the lower level of government, these jurisdictions can use the data to assess their own performance relative to others. Such data should also be made public, not only to keep citizens informed but also to enable citizens to encourage and support agency efforts for improvement. Exhibit 8-1 outlines steps for using CPM information to improve agency performance.

2. *Reward exceptional employee or organization performance.* If an agency is performing very well as compared with other agencies, officials should consider whether special recognition is appropriate. For example, Maryland uses CPM data on public school performance (see chapter 2) to identify those schools that will receive cash bonuses (Argetsinger 1999b). Agency officials should also consider whether the high level of performance is sufficiently important to warrant publicizing it not just internally but also to the community. Jurisdictions and agencies should certainly advertise their success stories, but as emphasized in chapter 7, they should also report instances where they have not been as successful.

3. *Create accountability.* Public sector managers often work with little or no information about their organizations' actual performance. Many managers rely heavily on their intuition, judgment, and experience. While valuable, these tools can be greatly enhanced and focused through good information. Comparative performance measurement provides points of reference that program managers can use to identify areas where their organization is performing well and those that need improvement. Agency officials should review their agency's standing on CPM indicators for each service for which they are responsible.

Assigning responsibility and creating accountability for achieving organizational goals are difficult at best. Comparative performance measurement helps achieve accountability by providing benchmarks from other similar agencies. Comparisons with jurisdictions that agency officials believe are most similar to themselves may be particularly useful for this purpose, but important insights can be gained from dissimilar agencies as well.

A key element of accountability includes making CPM information available to elected officials, to officials of agencies with responsibility for the services being compared, and to the general public. These individuals, with the help of CPM data, can hold agency management accountable for performance.

4. *Set targets for an organization's activities.* Agency staff often believe they and their organization are performing at or near their optimum level. They may believe this, in part, because they do not know the performance levels achieved by other similar organizations. As a result, most organizations are

EXHIBIT 8-1

Steps for Using CPM Information to Improve Your Agency's Performance

Step 1: Identify indicators where your agency's performance is lower than expected. This can be accomplished by reviewing the comparative information and identifying those indicators where your agency rates poorly.

Step 2: Determine which of the indicators reflect areas critical to the success of the agency. The performance indicators compared are likely to be of differing importance to the future success of your agency. When reviewing the indicators, focus on identifying a limited number of indicators that are most critical to the agency. Target your improvement efforts on those, rather than trying to address all areas at once.

Step 3: Identify causes of lower-than-expected results other than performance. Do not jump to conclusions before taking this step. Other causes might include incorrect data, special circumstances in your jurisdiction (unusual local economic or weather conditions), personnel problems, organizational changes, and so on. It is important to determine if poor results are simply a one-time anomaly before launching a full-scale performance improvement effort.

Step 4: Identify the gap in performance. For those indicators selected, identify the gap between the effectiveness of your agency and the best-performing agency. For example, if your agency takes 15 days to complete a process while the best-performing agency takes only 3 days, the performance gap is 12 days. Similarly, if your agency has satisfied clients 72 percent of the time, and the best-performing agency has satisfied clients 94 percent of the time, the performance gap is 22 percentage points.

Step 5: Determine reasons for the performance gaps, or enablers for improved performance. The reasons for the performance gaps are most often differences in how agencies operate, the tools they use, and the policies and processes they follow. For example, the best-performing agencies may all use an automated system to assist in completing a process. This system then becomes the reason, or enabler, for improved performance.

Step 6: Evaluate how adaptable the enablers are to your agency. Some reasons for improved performance can be easily adapted and applied to your agency. Others cannot be implemented because of differences in legal authority, in organizational structure and culture, or in the clients or community served. These factors should be considered when determining which performance improvements to implement in your agency.

Step 7: Establish performance improvement goals. Based on what you have learned from the previous steps, establish specific goals for improving the performance of your agency. For example, you may want to establish a goal of reducing the number of days required to complete a process.

Step 8: Implement performance improvement initiatives. This step includes committing the necessary resources, making the necessary changes in organizational structure or processes, and fully informing all agency personnel affected.

Step 9: Monitor, report, and celebrate performance improvements. As the performance improvement initiatives are implemented, track the results to ensure performance is moving in the right direction, report improvements throughout the agency, and celebrate the improvements to reinforce the benefits of change.

very conservative when setting targets, often designating levels very close to their current performance.

Comparing an agency's performance with other similar organizations provides agency officials with a broader perspective. It can make them aware that other organizations are performing at a substantially better level and that better performance *is* achievable. This, in turn, may motivate managers to be more aggressive in setting goals. For example, when Bureau of Finance staff in Norfolk, Virginia, looked at ICMA CPM Consortium data, they found they were not among the best-performing jurisdictions in terms of response time for emergency repairs to facilities. Data for FY 1996 showed that Norfolk had a 60-minute response time, while some other jurisdictions reported responding in 10 or 15 minutes. As a result of the broader perspective afforded by the comparative data, the Bureau made emergency response time a priority and response time was reduced to 31 minutes by FY 1998 (although it is not clear that specific targets were set to realize this improvement) (Bjornlund 1999, 34).

Managers can use CPM data to establish a variety of reasonable targets. For example, an agency whose reported values are well below the average values for a given indicator might choose to use as its target the *average* value of all the jurisdictions in recent comparison reports. Agencies that are performing at or above the average can use one of the higher values, or the *highest* value, as their target. Of course, other factors need to be considered, including the financial and staff resources available and special conditions present in the particular jurisdiction.

5. *Publicize the comparative data internally to motivate employees to achieve better results, or if the agency is already at the top, to motivate them to maintain that position.* Agencies should announce the results of the comparisons to all staff involved in providing the particular service. In some cases, agencies may be able to offer tangible rewards, such as a luncheon, plaque, or some other compensation, to help motivate employees. Agency performance might be considered in salary reviews or promotion decisions for employees whose work contributed to that performance. In some (usually rare) cases, such as the Maryland school example noted above, an entire agency may be rewarded with a bonus for its performance.

6. *Identify "successful" practices that other agencies use to improve performance.* One of the most difficult aspects of achieving organizational objectives is identifying what can be done to move the organization toward its goals. Identifying similar organizations with better outcomes can help managers to discover alternative strategies—this is frequently described as identifying "best practices." It may be more accurate to describe them, however, as "successful practices," since most CPM efforts do not really try to determine that certain practices or procedures really are better than others, or that they demonstrably result in superior performance.

While most CPM efforts do not seek "successful practices" information, ICMA's Local Government Consortium effort contacted high-performing agencies to obtain information about policies or practices they felt contributed to their high performance (see chapter 6). Brief descriptions of practices, provided by the jurisdictions, were included in the Consortium's FY 1995 and 1996 reports.

In addition, some Consortium jurisdictions sought specific information from each other apart from the successful practices information published by ICMA. For example, Bellevue, Washington, learned from the comparative data that its juvenile arrest rate was greater than that of comparable communities. Staff contacted other participants in the effort to obtain information on practices addressing juvenile crime. Bellevue also analyzed its own data more closely to better understand the characteristics of its juvenile offenders. These steps resulted in a new strategy to improve performance. The Police Department was restructured to create a Family Services Division staffed by police personnel who work with families, youth, and neighborhoods. In addition, as part of the city's effort to reduce juvenile crime, the Parks and Recreation Department initiated new programming for youth (Bjornlund 1999, 34–35).

While not all of the practices or procedures used by one agency will be adaptable to other agencies, some likely will be. Additionally, reviewing the strategies employed by comparable organizations may lead agency officials to use a combination of practices or to develop new strategies or procedures that build on the knowledge gained from others.

7. *Change organizational beliefs and behaviors.* Every organization operates with certain "myths" that are well accepted, but not really proven. For example, an agency may hold the belief that its employees have larger caseloads, that it has fewer resources, or that it is performing better than other similar organizations. These myths limit the amount of energy and creativity devoted to improving a service. For instance, the Long Beach Police Department functioned with a well-entrenched myth that its caseload per detective was much larger than similar departments, therefore explaining its lackluster performance in solving or clearing criminal cases. A comparison with other police departments in California showed that the caseload was actually smaller than most other departments. This information shattered the myth and allowed the organization to work toward improving its performance.

8. *Determine reasonable workload levels and resource needs.* Many CPM efforts provide information on the resources used to provide a service and the workload of each employee. This comparative information can be used to determine whether too few or too many resources are committed to a particular service and to help adjust workload levels if necessary. For example, the City of Winston-Salem, North Carolina, discovered from the comparative data provided by the Institute of Government's CPM effort that its cost per ton for refuse collection was very high relative to the other cities. Previous to the effort, Winston-Salem had been using a task system that allowed employees to go home when the collection routes were finished. As a result of the CPM effort, officials discovered that many of the collection routes did not include enough homes, explaining why its costs were higher than other cities (Coe 1999). This information led the city to make adjustments to the routes in order to reduce its costs.

9. *Improve communications with elected officials.* Comparative performance measurement can be an effective way to promote better decisionmaking among

elected officials regarding policies and resource allocation. It is often surprising how little information is available to our elected officials for use in making decisions. Often they know little more than that a problem needs to be addressed and frequently are left with only one option—allocate more resources. More often than not, this is not the best decision. In contrast, agency officials may know what policy or resource decisions other jurisdictions have made, but lack information on how well those decisions have worked.

Several jurisdictions participating in the ICMA CPM Consortium made special efforts to share CPM data with elected officials. City staff in Austin, Texas, and Riverside, California, distributed copies of the annual ICMA *Data Report* to each council member. Riverside staff wrote a cover memo that explained the project, cautioned about data accuracy and interpretation, and identified key findings. Austin staff conducted briefings for elected officials. CPM data also were presented in budget documents in a number of jurisdictions. In order to help elected officials use the CPM data, staff in Bellevue, Washington, developed a separate report explaining basic terms and summarizing key findings for 27 indicators they had selected as the most important from a policy perspective. The comparative bar charts from the ICMA *Data Report* were presented for each of these indicators, along with a brief description of "what the data mean to us" and "next steps." An executive summary highlighted key findings and planned actions. For example, in a summary of 1996 police data, the report noted Bellevue's relatively high juvenile arrest rate and plans to reallocate resources to form a Family and Youth Services Unit (Bjornlund 1999, 19–21).

Dakota County, Minnesota, exemplifies elected officials' use of CPM data for resource allocation and policymaking. In their review of the ICMA CPM data, county officials discovered that the county had a lower percentage of paved roads than comparable counties. This information stimulated the county supervisors to review road paving policies and initiate a study to determine if they should focus on paving more county roads (Bjornlund 1999, 34).

10. *Communicate with the public.* To improve public trust in public service agencies, citizens need credible information on service outcomes. As discussed in chapter 7, even if the comparisons reveal poor performance, that information should be available to citizens. (Preferably, poorly performing agencies should also identify current or planned actions for performance improvement.)

The current era is most definitely focused on the consumer. Consumers, and the media, increasingly expect "consumer report"–type information on goods and services—including those provided by government and nonprofit service agencies. Comparative performance measurement helps governments provide this type of information. The community gains a better understanding of what is being accomplished with tax dollars and a greater sense of value received for those taxes. CPM may also help citizens understand what new value could be received from an additional investment, even a tax increase. For example, a comparison of road quality conducted among several adjacent communities may reveal that the road quality in a given community is much worse than in the surrounding communities. Officials in the one community discover that surrounding communities spend much more on their roads—money raised through a special road tax. By communicating this information to the public, community leaders can make citizens aware of the trade-offs between price and quality, enabling them to decide if lower taxes or better roads provide the better value.

Such comparisons can also be used to identify areas that need attention within the community. Government officials might use CPM information to encourage citizens to help government agencies improve service performance. Most government outcomes are not solely the result of government actions. The things citizens do, or do *not* do, contribute to performance achieved in many areas. Refuse collection and street-cleaning activities are typical examples. A community's streets are likely to be cleaner if citizens place their refuse in appropriate containers and avoid littering.

Some jurisdictions that participated in the ICMA CPM Consortium made explicit efforts to communicate comparative data to the public. As noted above, some jurisdictions included these data in budget documents, one mechanism used to communicate with the public. Other communities went beyond that. Both Kansas City, Missouri, and Portland, Oregon, posted some CPM data on their Web sites. Staff in Long Beach, California, presented CPM data at community meetings to give citizens a broader perspective from which to assess city services. Long Beach also incorporated CPM data into its annual report of performance measures, *Hitting the Mark*. Furthermore, a new section was added to that report—"Raising the Bar"—which presented comparative data for 10 ICMA Consortium jurisdictions that closely resemble Long Beach in population and geographic size. Similarly, Portland, Oregon's *Service Efforts and Accomplishments* report (produced annually by the Auditor's Office), while primarily focusing on internal performance measures, also provided comparative data for six similar cities. The city also produced a condensed (four-page) version of the report, including some comparison data, to make performance measurement information more user-friendly and citizen accessible (Bjornlund 1999).

To date, it appears that relatively few communities use CPM data in their citizen involvement efforts. The ICMA CPM effort sponsored workshops on performance measurement for interested citizens in member jurisdictions, and approximately 16 jurisdictions in the Consortium participated in these workshops (Bjornlund 1999, 27; Kopczynski and Lombardo 1999; National Civic League and the Urban Institute 1999). The workshops (supported by grant funds from the Sloan Foundation) provided training to help citizen groups better understand CPM information and its usefulness in furthering their work and in holding governments accountable. In some communities, these workshops were aimed at ongoing efforts, such as strategic planning, that involve citizens. Other jurisdictions used these workshops as springboards for citizen involvement. Tucson, Arizona, launched its community visioning process through the workshops, and Phoenix used the workshops to initiate a series of public meetings focused on identifying community priorities and developing performance indicators for these priorities (Bjornlund 1999, 38–39).

A Final Note

A special note on private, nonprofit service organizations: Encouraged by such national associations as the United Way of America, many local service organizations are beginning to introduce outcome measurement. National associations and their members are beginning to think in terms of obtaining common data from members in order to encourage improvements and identify successful practices. This is expected to be a major growth area for CPM over the next decade.

Clearly, there are many ways in which CPM can contribute to improving the services provided by government and nonprofit organizations. When considering the use of CPM, the outlook of involved agency officials is key. As David Ammons (1999) has suggested, officials should avoid a defensive attitude toward CPM, even though comparison is likely to create anxiety. Managers who focus on "What can I learn?" and "How can we use what we learn to make our services better?" are likely to feel more comfortable about CPM and make good use of the information obtained. And, ultimately, the public will benefit.

References

Ammons, David N. 1999. "A Proper Mentality for Benchmarking." *Public Administration Review* 59 (2): 105–109.

Annie E. Casey Foundation. 1998. *Kids Count Data Book: State Profiles of Child Well-Being.* Baltimore, Md.: Annie E. Casey Foundation.

Argetsinger, Amy. 1999a. "Beating Poverty in the Classroom." *Washington Post*, 16 May, p. C5.

———. 1999b. "Scores Drop for First Time in Maryland School Exams." *Washington Post*, 2 December.

Barrett, Katherine, and Richard Greene. 1999. "Grading the States: A Management Report Card." *Governing* (February): 17–90.

Bjornlund, Lydia. 1999. *Beyond Data: Current Uses of Comparative Performance Measurement in Local Government.* Washington, D.C.: International City/County Management Association Center for Performance Measurement.

Bjornlund, Lydia, and Derek Okubo. 1999. *Engaging Citizens: Citizen Involvement in Community Performance.* Denver, Colo.: National Civic League.

Coe, Charles. 1999. "Local Government Benchmarking: Lessons from Two Major Multigovernment Efforts." *Public Administration Review* 59 (2): 111–15.

Few, Paula K., and A. John Vogt. 1997. "Measuring the Performance of Local Governments." *Popular Government* 62 (2): 41–54.

Fink, Arlene, and Jacqueline Kosecoff. 1998. *How to Conduct Surveys: A Step-by-Step Guide.* 2d ed. Thousand Oaks, Calif.: Sage Publications.

Georgia, State of. Department of Community Affairs. 1999. "Community Indicators User Guide." http://www.dca.state.ga.us/commind/guide.asp.

Goldstein, Barry (Director, Division of Women's and Children's Health). 1998. Interview by Harry Hatry and Elisa Vinson of the Urban Institute. 2 October.

Gormley, William T., Jr. 1998. "Assessing Health Care Report Cards." *Journal of Public Administration Research and Theory* 8 (3): 325–52.

Gormley, William T., Jr., and David L. Weimer. 1999. *Organizational Report Cards*. Cambridge, Mass.: Harvard University Press.

Greiner, John M. 1994. "Use of Ratings by Trained Observers." In *Handbook of Practical Program Evaluation*, edited by Joseph S. Wholey, Harry P. Hatry, and Kathryn E. Newcomer. San Francisco, Calif.: Jossey-Bass Publishers.

Hatry, Harry P. 1999. *Performance Measurement: Getting Results*. Washington, D.C.: The Urban Institute Press.

Hatry, Harry P., and Mary Kopczynski. 1997. *Guide to Program Outcome Measurement for the U.S. Department of Education*. Washington, D.C.: U.S. Department of Education. February.

Hatry, Harry P., John E. Marcotte, Thérèse van Houten, and Carol H. Weiss. 1998. *Customer Surveys for Agency Managers: What Managers Need to Know*. Washington, D.C.: The Urban Institute Press.

ICMA. See International City/County Management Association.

International City/County Management Association (ICMA). 1997. *Comparative Performance Measurement: FY 1995 Data Report*. Washington, D.C.: ICMA.

———. 1998. *Comparative Performance Measurement: FY 1996 Data Report*. Washington, D.C.: ICMA.

———. 1999a. *Comparative Performance Measurement: FY 1997 Data Report*. Washington, D.C.: ICMA.

———. 1999b. *Comparative Performance Measurement: FY 1998 Data Report*. Washington, D.C.: ICMA.

Kopczynski, Mary, and Michael Lombardo. 1999. "Comparative Performance Measurement: Insights and Lessons Learned from a Consortium Effort." *Public Administration Review* (59) 2: 124–34.

Lemann, Nicholas. 1999. "America's Best Colleges." *U.S. News & World Report*. http://www.usnews.com/usnews/edu/college/rankings/coschool.htm.

Long Beach (Calif.), City of. Auditor's Office. 1994. *Long Beach Police Department Strategic Plan Peer Comparison Report*. February.

Maryland Higher Education Commission. 1999. *1998 Performance Accountability Report: Maryland Public Colleges and Universities*. Annapolis, Md.: Maryland Higher Education Commission. November.

Minnesota, State of. Office of the Legislative Auditor. 1998. *9-1-1 Dispatching: A Best Practices Review*. St. Paul, Minn.: State of Minnesota.

Money. 2000. "The Best Places to Live in America." http://www.money.com/money/depts/real_estate/bestplaces.

Murphey, David A. 1998. *1998 Community Profile Report*. Waterbury: Vermont Agency of Human Services, Planning Division. November.

———. 1999. "Presenting Community-Level Data in an 'Outcomes and Indicators' Framework: Lessons from Vermont's Experience." *Public Administration Review* 59 (1): 76–82.

National Civic League and the Urban Institute. 1999. *A Model for Community-Based Workshops on Performance Measurement*. Denver, Colo.: National Civic League.

North Carolina Local Government Performance Measurement Project. 1997. *Performance and Cost Data: Phase I—City Services.* Chapel Hill: Institute of Government, The University of North Carolina at Chapel Hill. October.

North Carolina, State of. Department of Health and Human Services. 1998. *Women's Preventive Health Program Rankings for Fiscal Year 1996–1997.* Raleigh: State of North Carolina.

Reingold, Jennifer. 1998. "The Best B-Schools." *Business Week,* 8 October.

Rubin, Allen, and Earl Babbie. 1997. *Research Methods for Social Work.* 3d ed. Pacific Grove, Calif.: Brooks/Cole.

Savageau, David, with Ralph D'Agostino. 1999. *Places Rated Almanac—Millennium Edition.* Foster City, Calif.: IDG Books Worldwide, Inc.

Schmidt, William H., and Curtis C. McKnight. 1998. "What Can We Really Learn from TIMSS?" *Science* 282 (December 4): 1830–31.

Takahira, Sayuri, Patrick Gonzales, Mary Frase, and Laura Hersh Salganik. 1998. *Pursuing Excellence: A Study of U.S. Twelfth-Grade Mathematics and Science Achievement in International Context—Initial Findings from the Third International Mathematics and Science Study (TIMSS).* Washington, D.C.: National Center for Education Statistics. February.

Tufte, Edward R. 1992. *The Visual Display of Quantitative Information.* Cheshire, Conn.: Graphics Press.

United Kingdom. Audit Commission. 1999. *Feedback 98: Results of the Commission's Consultation on the Local Authority Performance Indicators for 1999/2000.* London.

U.S. Department of Education. National Center for Education Statistics. 1998. *Pursuing Excellence: A Study of U.S. Twelfth-Grade Mathematics and Science Achievement in International Context.* Washington, D.C.: U.S. Government Printing Office.

U.S. Department of Transportation. Office of Aviation Enforcement and Proceedings. 2000. "Air Travel Consumer Report." http://www.dot.gov/airconsumer/index1.htm. (Accessed October 11, 2000.)

Waters Boots, Shelley. 1999. *State Child Welfare Spending at a Glance: A Supplemental Report to the Cost of Protecting Vulnerable Children.* Washington, D.C.: The Urban Institute. June.

Weeks, Dale. 1997a. *Performance Measurement Benchmarking Project, Pilot Product and Service Test Plan, State Tax Agency Feedback Response Package.* Washington, D.C.: Federation of Tax Administrators. 21 April.

———. 1997b. *Performance Measurement Benchmarking Project, Strategic Tax Management Processes and Representative Performance Measurements.* Washington, D.C.: Federation of Tax Administrators. September/October.

Wolfe, Ann F. (North Carolina Department of Health and Human Services). 1998. Memo on program ranks to local health directors. 8 April.

Additional Readings

Ammons, David N. 1996. *Municipal Benchmarks: Assessing Local Performance and Establishing Community Standards.* Thousand Oaks, Calif.: Sage Publications.

Fund for the City of New York. Center on Municipal Government Performance. 1998. *How Smooth Are New York City's Streets?* New York: Fund for the City of New York. September.

United Way of America. 1996. *Measuring Program Outcomes: A Practical Approach.* Alexandria, Va.: United Way of America.

U.S. Department of Education. Office of Educational Research and Improvement. 1996. *Reading Literacy in the United States: Findings from the IEA Reading Literacy Study.* Washington, D.C.: National Center for Education Statistics.

Index

targets for organizations' activities, setting, 92, 94

tax collection, 26

Third International Mathematics and Science Study (TIMSS), 17–18, 71, 72, 86, 87

time periods, indicators involving, 46

time trends, 65

timeliness, as vital for usefulness, 47

timing and timeliness problems, 47

Total Quality Management (TQM), 5

Transportation, Department of, 10

U

unit-cost ratio. *See* efficiency ratio

Uniform Crime Reports, 11, 20, 41, 44, 57

United Kingdom (U.K.) local authority performance indicators, 20–21

U.S. News's "America's best colleges," 11, 13–14

V

Vermont's Agency of Human Services (AHS) "Community Profiles," 21–22, 60

outcome indicators used by, 38, 42

voluntary CPM efforts, 34. *See also* cooperative (self-initiated) comparisons

W

"weighting" each indicator, 66

women's preventive health care rankings, 68

workload level, determining reasonable, 95

About the Authors

Elaine Morley is a senior research associate in the Public Management Program of the Urban Institute's Metropolitan Housing and Communities Center. She has had considerable experience in projects involving performance measurement and public services and was recently involved in an assessment of outcome measurement in nonprofit organizations. She has also been involved in the evaluation of national programs for at-risk youth. Prior to joining the Institute, Dr. Morley served as an associate professor of public administration and policy analysis at Southern Illinois University at Edwardsville.

Scott Bryant is principal of Scott P. Bryant & Associates, which provides consulting services in strategic planning, organizational improvement, quality management, and performance measurement to local governments. Prior to starting his firm, he served as the director of strategic management for Long Beach, California, and was manager of public sector consulting with Ernst & Young in Washington, D.C., and southern California. Mr. Bryant has also conducted management and organizational studies of state government departments and programs for the Colorado Legislature and managed two federal demonstration programs for the Denver Mayor's Office. He is a frequent speaker at conferences on performance measurement and has taught numerous workshops for local governments on performance measurement, strategic management, benchmarking, performance-based budgeting, and community-oriented public safety.

Harry Hatry is a principal research associate at the Urban Institute, where he is the director of the Institute's Public Management Program. Since the early 1970s, he has been a leader in developing procedures that allow nonprofit organizations and federal, state, and local government agencies to track how well they are performing their services. In recent years, he has also worked to improve performance measurement and management in other countries, including Thailand and Hungary. He has authored or coauthored numerous books, reports, and articles describing performance measurement procedures, including publications for the U.S. Departments of Education and Justice, the International City/County Management Association, and United Way of America. Key works in which he has been an author include *How Effective Are Your Community Services? Procedures for Measuring Their Quality; Practical Program Evaluation for State and Local Governments; Program Analysis for State and Local Governments;* and *Performance Measurement.* He has received awards relating to his work in performance measurement and evaluation from a number of organizations, including the American Society for Public Administration and the National Academy of Public Administration.